Ferrari 308 Series

BUYER'S GUIDE
&
OWNER'S GUIDE

by

Steve Cook

Visit ~ www.308book.com ~ for
updated information on this book and others.

INTRODUCTION

Welcome to the world of digital publishing ~ the book you now hold in your hand, published by **VelocePress,** was printed using the latest state of the art digital technology. The advent of print-on-demand has forever changed the publishing process, never has information been so accessible and it is our hope that this book serves your informational needs for years to come. If this is your first exposure to digital publishing, we hope that you are pleased with the results. Many more titles of interest to the classic automobile and motorcycle enthusiast are available via our website at **www.VelocePress.com.** We hope that you find this title as interesting as we do.

SPECIAL THANKS

We would like to take this opportunity to extend our thanks to everyone who contributed to the preparation of this book, in particular to **Lynn Getz** of **VelocePress** for her perseverance in editing the original manuscript.

NOTE FROM THE PUBLISHER

The information presented is true and complete to the best of our knowledge. All recommendations are made without any guarantees on the part of the author or the publisher, who also disclaim all liability incurred with the use of this information.

TRADEMARKS

We recognize that some words, model names and designations, for example, mentioned herein are the property of the trademark holder. We use them for identification purposes only. This is not an official publication.

INFORMATION ON THE USE OF THIS PUBLICATION

In today's information age we are constantly subject to changes in common practice, new technology, availability of improved materials and increased awareness of chemical toxicity. As such, it is advised that the user consult with an experienced professional prior to undertaking any procedure described herein. While every care has been taken to ensure correctness of information, it is obviously not possible to guarantee complete freedom from errors or omissions or to accept liability arising from such errors or omissions. Therefore, any individual that uses the information contained within, or elects to perform or participate in do-it-yourself repairs or modifications acknowledges that there is a risk factor involved and that the publisher or its associates cannot be held responsible for personal injury or property damage resulting from the use of the information or the outcome of such procedures.

It is important that the reader recognizes that any instructions may refer to either the right-hand or left-hand sides of the vehicle or the components and that the directions are followed carefully. One final word of advice, this publication is intended to be used as a reference guide, and when in doubt the reader should consult with a qualified **Ferrari** expert.

INDEX

Ferrari 308 Buyer's and Owner's Guide

CHAPTER 1

Introduction

My first personal experience with a Ferrari was as a passenger in a 1981 308 GTSi. The car was clad in the usual red with tan leather interior. It was early August in 1984, and even though this happened almost 25 years ago, I still remember it as vividly as many of the most important events in my life - my wedding day, the day our son was born, my 21st birthday (okay, so I don't remember that day very well).

It was a warm summer day in Albuquerque when one of my friends dropped by and told me that someone was coming over to his house to show off her new Ferrari. Like most teenage boys, I was familiar enough with cars to know that a Ferrari was something special. I wasn't going to miss it!

We rushed back to my friend's house and waited in the front yard. We glanced up and down the street with anticipation, hoping that each car turning the corner would be it. We'd hear a car around the bend and our hopes would get higher, only to be dashed when we realized it was some other normal and boring car.

Then we heard it. It wasn't loud like a racecar, but it was unmistakably different from all the cars we'd ever heard. We knew it was coming. We could feel it. We rushed toward the street hoping to get a glimpse of it sooner.

The 308 glided around the corner and headed toward us. It was smaller than we expected - and lower, as if it was hovering just above the ground. Yet it was so mesmerizing, neither of us could take our eyes off of it. Even from a distance the red paint was gorgeous.

The Ferrari pulled slowly into the driveway. The exhaust was loud, deep and overwhelming. It resonated in my chest as if my whole body felt the car breathing. When the driver stopped in front of the house and shut the car off, the noise went away instantly but the feeling was still there. The car was awe-inspiring.

There were several of us standing around ogling the vehicle. The top was off and the windows were down. The driver shouted, "Who wants a ride?" Everyone shouted but in the end, the older guys went first, and we had to wait for our turn.

Thirty minutes later it was finally my turn for a ride. I realized just how low the 308 was as I plopped inside with little grace. I put my belt on while she asked if I'd ever been in a Ferrari. I told her that I hadn't and she replied, "Then you're in for something special!"

"Yeah," was the best response I could come up with as I took in the sights and sounds of the 308's interior. She continued: "A Ferrari is unlike any other car in the world. It's not just the looks and style. Each Ferrari has a history of passion and SOUL." She stressed the word "soul", and it stuck in my head.

A car with soul? How could that be? How can a car have soul? It wasn't until I owned my first 308 years later that I fully understood. The history of Ferrari is unlike that of any other carmaker. Of course I didn't realize any of that as we zipped past a public park where kids and adults were out enjoying the day. They all seemed to look over at us cruising by at a leisurely pace. They could hear the unique exhaust note. A glimpse of red would catch their eye and they would instinctively look up at us. The only thing that came to my mind was "All these people see the car. It must be the soul!" I didn't say it out loud, but that's what I kept thinking. "This car gets lots of attention," she said. I could only nod in agreement.

We finally exited the residential area and pulled out onto a major street. Although the GTSi is recognized as the least powerful of all 308s, it's no slouch. And when she punched it, a grin spread across my face that went from ear to ear. The noise, the gentle push back into the firm leather seat, and the beautiful noise!

We moved along quickly and approached an intersection. She put her blinker on, in preparation for the 90 degree right turn. At the speed we were going, I assumed we were going to take the next intersection, and that she was just putting the turn signal on early. Then she did it. With amazing precision, she made the 308 dive into the turn. I had to lean into the corner to keep from falling over. The 308 took the corner so smoothly and confidently that it took my breath away. "Because the car is so low," she shouted over the engine noise, "it can turn very quickly!" All I could do was grin in response.

The next stop light was red, and she didn't seem to notice. She approached with her foot still firmly planted on the gas pedal. My muscles tensed and I cried out, "It's red!"

"I know," she replied. A few seconds later when I figured she was just going to run through the intersection, she started pressing the brakes with bold intention. The car responded by slowing down so quickly I was thrown against the seat-belt. The tires held fast, and only let out a short screech of protest.

That was the start of my Ferrari obsession. Posters, magazines, models - you name it, I had it or wanted it. Then, in 1986, Ferris Bueller's Day Off hit the movie theaters. Even though it was a 250GT California Spyder, instead of a 308, the scene in Cameron's father's garage effectively portrayed the passion and soul in the Ferrari automobiles. It's my contention that movies like Ferris Bueller and television shows like Magnum P.I. and Miami Vice all helped spark the outrageously high Ferrari Market of the late 80's!

Since my first encounter, I've owned a couple of 308s, driven dozens, ridden in a hundred or so, and drooled over thousands more. Though some Ferraristi still consider the 308 as a "starter Ferrari" or "poor man's Ferrari", it is still one of the most popular and recognizable Ferraris models ever. It makes an excellent introduction to the marque, and even though it's the most common Ferrari, each example is unique and special by virtue of the prancing horse on the hood.

A PRIMER ON PASSION AND SOUL

As I have mentioned, my friend with the Ferrari emphatically declared that each Ferrari has a history, passion, and soul.

History we understand, passion can at least be defined, but soul? Is this not just some motorhead psycho-babble? Or do cars, those inanimate, cold creations of man, really have something which could be defined as soul?

Define an automotive soul and one can perhaps explain the Ferrari mystique. And while Ferrari historians must shy away from speaking in such terms for fear of sounding like Shirley MacLaine, we are free from such restraints. But forget about Ferrari for a minute. Other cars have soul, too. How about a Lamborghini? Corvette? Model T? Porsche? MGTC? Jag XKE? A Rolls Royce Silver Ghost? Bugatti (no question mark here). What elements do these cars have in common? And how does Ferrari rate with the competition?

The Creator
One of the most commonly shared elements is a strong, individual designer or constructor/industrialist. The Ford Model T was truly Henry's baby, although many others had a hand in its creation and it was mass produced.

The Jaguar XKE reflected the will of William Lyons and his staff. The Silver Ghost was a direct result of Henry Royce's dreams, the Lamborghini was Ferruccio's concept. And even when the original instigators are gone, the spirit, the intent, the direction, often lives on, at least for a while, as in the case of Porsche, the post-war MGs, Morgans and Corvette. The original Mini was the almost sole creation of Alex Issigonis, which is why the real Mini has soul and the new Mini does not.

Enzo Ferrari was perhaps the strongest, most complex, enigmatic and successful automobile constructor of the twentieth century.

Individuality

Another element is individuality. There can be no mistaking an XKE from either inside the car or from the outside. The same can be said for the Silver Ghost, Model T or any car with soul. Even blindfolded, an enthusiast can instantly identify each car by its sound, feel, smell, touch.

The cars of Enzo Ferrari were not only unique as models, but until recently, unique in themselves. Individuality personified. Much of the cult of individuality has carried forth into the 21st century. There is nothing like a Ferrari.

Desirability

Desirability is also shared among cars with soul, even if mass produced and available to a large population. Make it available only to a few and the desirability factor increases accordingly.

Ferraris are not only desired by the masses, who cannot afford one, but both old and new Ferraris are eagerly sought by captains of industry, royalty, movie stars, old money, and new money in every nation in the world. The degree of desirability has no bounds.

Primary motivation

In most cases one will find that money was not the prime reason for the production of significant cars. Henry Ford wanted to supply the masses with an inexpensive and durable automobile. Zora Arkus Duntov wanted to create the only real American sports car in the Corvette. Henry Royce wanted to build the best car in the world. In fact, many of the world's most desirable cars never made any money for their companies, and in many cases caused the inevitable bankruptcy. Cars with soul are often envisioned, built and/or designed by men with a passion for automobiles, and are not concerned with profits.

The desire to build successful racing cars was so great that Ferrari nearly went bankrupt on several occasions. For him, money represented the means to build race cars. Today, Ferrari race cars are still successful in a variety of competitions, and winning races remains a top priority for the company.

Tradition and Location

Tradition and location also play a part. The Morgan is a good example of a car which strictly adheres to three generations of craftsmanship, and never left their original premises. Jaguars were built, and are still built, in Coventry, while the Corvette is still a US built fiberglass bodied V-8, as it has been since 1955. Tradition and stable location ensures that there is continuity in both the history and the workforce.

Ferraris have been constructed on the same premises since 1947. Many Ferrari employees are second and third generation employees. Ferrari is local, and although owned by Fiat, continues to create and build cars within the very same (although hugely expanded) framework which has existed for 57 years. In this era of the world car, Ferraris are still uniquely Italian.

Racing

Perhaps one of the most important aspects of the automotive soul is participation in racing. Like nothing else, racing generates passion, victory generates enthusiasm and pride. Automakers thrive on racing, even though some don't admit it. Leave out the racing part of the equation and one has a lesser automobile. The failure of Lamborghini to compete successfully with Ferrari is not due to a lesser product; many have proven far superior to Ferraris. Lamborghini has not achieved Ferrari status primarily because it has not participated in racing successfully.

Racing was the reason Ferrari automobiles were created and produced. Ferraris were built to race, and win. This they have been doing since 1947. Here only Porsche and Mercedes-Benz come close, but their lack of a long term presence in Formula 1 is a notable downside.

All of this adds up to passion, that human emotion which can be applied to both man made and natural creations. And therefore, soul.

ABOUT THIS BOOK

My love of Ferraris, and of the 308 specifically, is what prompted me to write this book. Since founding the FerrariList (the world's largest online Ferrari e-mail discussion list) almost a decade ago, I've read and saved a lot of Ferrari-related information. I've compiled much of that information, as well as information from numerous other sources, to create this book.

Who Should Read This Book
This book is written primarily for new 308 buyers and owners, but it should also be useful to long-time 308 owners who want to get a little more out of their car. Car nuts, Ferrari-fans and anyone that has dreamed of owning a Ferrari should find this book interesting. It answers many of the questions people have about Ferrari ownership.

How to Use This Book
I've divided this book into three sections: pre-purchase, purchase, and ownership. Each section is targeted to different stages of 308 ownership.

Pre-Purchase
A short history of Ferrari automobiles and the various 308 models will help you decide which 308 would best fit your needs and desires.

Purchase
How to find a 308 to purchase, including where to look, what to look for, how to protect yourself from costly mistakes and the best ways to go about purchasing the car you've found.

Ownership
How to undertake simple do-it-yourself maintenance and modifications you can make to improve your Ferrari. If you already own a 308, skip directly to this section, then refer to the first 2 sections if you'd like to see what you may have missed when you bought your car.

Opinions
As you could probably guess, every Ferrari owner has his or her own opinion on every aspect of Ferrari and their cars. So, don't be alarmed that some opinions appear in this book. I have made an effort to note when there are alternative points of view. In any case, this book should serve as a starting point for you to form your own opinions.

There are hundreds of anecdotal stories and urban legends about 308s and Ferraris in general. While most of these are based at least a little in fact, don't believe everything you hear.

Technical Notes

The skills needed to complete many of these procedures can confound even an experienced shade-tree mechanic. So in short, if you don't have the skills to do it already, this book won't be much help.

If you decide to work on your Ferrari, I can only offer you caution. One of the biggest pitfalls to working on your own Ferrari is the potential cost of mistakes. With most other cars, mistakes tend to be inexpensive, and your major problem is the time it takes to undo and repeat the procedure the correct way. But with a Ferrari, the stakes are much higher. Some mistakes could cost upwards of $10,000 to repair.

BUYING AND OWNING A FERRARI 308

You in A Ferrari?

Believe it or not, most people find it difficult to see themselves in a Ferrari. They assume that they are too expensive to purchase or impossible to maintain. Granted, these aren't "Italian Toyotas". They are true exotic cars that will need more attention than your usual everyday vehicle. But still, if you take the time and effort to find a good car and spend regular but minimal amounts of time and money to keep the car in good shape, ownership can be easy, affordable, and very enjoyable.

Pros and Cons

Even though a Ferrari 308 probably isn't the most expensive thing you'll ever buy, it is a large expense. And like other large expenses, especially ones that are for entertainment purposes, you should weigh the pros and cons of owning a Ferrari.

The 308 isn't your basic grocery-getter. You'll need to take better care of it than a modern daily driver. It's as simple as that. It needs your attention and if you don't provide it, it will come back to bite you - usually in the form of stranding you by the side of the road and a whopping repair bill.

Owning a 308 is also a commitment. You have to pay attention to it or you'll end up costing yourself a great deal of money. You can avoid the notoriously high repair fees if you buy yourself some insurance in the form of proper and timely maintenance.

There are many false rumors about the 308 being horribly expensive to own, but with a committed owner, the ownership costs can be quite reasonable.

The 308 isn't a muscle car by any stretch of the imagination. While it can certainly hold its own, it wasn't meant for drag racing in a straight line. It has a small capacity (3 liter) engine with a very low center of gravity. Handling is where the 308 shines, and that handling is emphasized by the fact that you're doing it in style.

A Ferrari 308 always gets noticed. This can be a pro or con depending on your personal preference but, be prepared, because you're going to get a lot of attention. Complete strangers will approach you at gas stations, stare at you as you pass by, drive in your blind spot for miles on end while they ogle, and tail-gate you as they try to get a better look at your car.

After reading this book, my goal is that you should be familiar enough with the risks and rewards of owning a 308 to decide for yourself if it's worth the time, trouble, and expense.

INVESTMENT POTENTIAL

What are 308s worth now, what will be worth when you are ready to sell, and what will they be worth in the future? Should you leave it to your estate? Should you buy low and try to sell high? Or just sit back and enjoy?

Long Term Investment
There are many elements here. But the first and most important to remember is the market is e mobile---like the song, Il Donna e Mobile. It is fickle. It will always be fickle. If we could predict the market, we'd all be rich and you could afford a GTO, not a 308.

The upside is that Ferraris have already had their day in the sun. The great Ferrari speculative boom which took place from 1985 to 1993 is in the past. For the potential 308 buyer, it means that the market is stable, and has been stable for roughly the past 10 years. You will pay little more now for a good 308 than you could have in 1995. For the foreseeable future, prices will probably remain level as well.

There is, however, a caveat here. Assuming the age of a potential Ferrari 308 buyer is in the range of 45-60 years old, the market for 308s has a bit of time to mature yet.

Why is this?
Speculators aside, we know that most people become interested in cars between the ages of 5 and 15 years old. Be it fishing, hunting, baseball or automobiles, the passion starts young. Imagine this scenario. In 1980 a ten year old boy watched the first episode of Magnum PI, and was entranced by the 308GTS driven by Tom Selleck.

Thirty or forty years later, after a successful career and having paid for his children's college, our TV viewer is ready to invest in a hobby. The fascination with the Magnum 308 re-occurs and he begins to look around.

So, should we assume that sometime after the year 2010, when our Ferraristi is forty, prices of 308s will suddenly start to surge? Perhaps, depending on the state of the economy. But perhaps there weren't many youngsters turned on by 308s in the first place!

Another element is the rise of Asiatic countries such as China. As the new industrial might creates new millionaires, we might expect to see a flood of Chinese invading the market, buying up old Ferraris and creating another boom.

This happened with the Japanese in the 1980s. But are the Chinese likely to do the same? The culture, and history of Korea, Indochina and China are simply not similar to that of Japan; to make the assumption that they are economic clones ignores history and environment.

Remember, the market is fickle and dependent on many events out of our control or even imagination. If you buy a Ferrari today, and are very, very lucky and, in the end, you might break even.

Short Term investment
Short term (3-6 years) investment potential depends heavily on two facts, assuming the market stays stable:

1. how much you paid for the car originally
2. how much you put into the car during ownership

Sounds simple, doesn't it. But let's assume you bought a 308 in really good shape at current market value with recent servicing that included timing belts, water pump (oh, yes, they do go!) and cam adjustment. At the very least, before you sell, you will have to do it again. DIY and you're in for around $1,500, have someone else do it and you're looking at $3-5,000.
Add miscellaneous maintenance, (tires? Ouch. Exhaust system? Ooohh) insurance costs, and you'll have up to $10,000 into your Ferrari -- in addition to the entry cost. Adding mileage to the car does not help resale value and, conversely, having it sit in the garage for 6 years means that seals, brakes, shocks, and all sort of assorted gaskets will have to be replaced. A no win situation.

Being realistic, therefore, Ferrari 308 ownership over a 5-6 year period is going to cost you money, not make you money. This is a truth. Assuming otherwise is a failure of logic and simple math. But, if you compare the cost with the purchase of a new car and it's depreciation of 30-40% in the first two years, it's not a bad deal.

So, as you read through this book, write down your own list of pros and cons to make sure that the upsides outweigh the downsides of owning your own Ferrari 308.

CHAPTER 2 *History and Passion*

FERRARI HISTORY

As you already know, the history of Ferrari is long and distinguished. From its beginnings as a race team for Alfa Romeo to its most recent exotic supercars, the spirit of Ferrari runs through everything it has created and accomplished.

Every Ferrari owner, future owner, or Ferrari fan should be familiar with the important events of Ferrari's existence. The history of Ferrari is part of what makes these automobiles so special and by understanding the history, you can enjoy your car on a completely different level.

There are literally hundreds of books published about Enzo Ferrari and the history of Ferrari automobiles. Books are available with topics as general as the complete history or as specific as entire books focusing on a single car. For those readers interested in knowing more about the history of Ferrari, there is a list of books given at the end of this chapter.

The history of Ferrari can be divided into four distinct eras: The Formative years, 1899-1945, the Golden Era, from 1945-1970, A Changing World, from 1970-1988, and The Fiat Era, from 1990 to the present.

1899-1945: The Formative Years

Enzo Ferrari was born on February 18th, 1898 to a family in Modena that could perhaps be called middle class. The Ferraris, though not rich, were certainly not poor. "My father came from Capri, a village near Modena and my mother's family was from Forli. We lived in a modest house out in the suburbs; four rooms over my father's metal working business," wrote Enzo, in his book "Una Vita Per l'Automobile" (A Life of Automobiles).

Enzo's father and older brother were "always talking about cars", and at the age of

10, his father took him to a motor race in Bologna, won by Felice Nazzaro. From that time on, Enzo Ferrari knew he wanted to be involved with racing cars. In 1916, young Enzo suffered the tragic loss of both his older brother and father. Ferrari entered service in the Italian army and served in an Alpine Artillery outfit until 1918. After his discharge, living on the small inheritance left by his father, Ferrari eventually found a job as a test driver with a small firm called CMN. Later, he began racing them, with enough success to purchase a Isotta-Fraschini. This led to a drive in an Alfa Romeo, in which he placed second at the grueling Targa Florio in 1920. He then drove Alfa Romeos with a fair amount of success throughout the twenties. During this time Ferrari began to associate himself with a number of wealthy men who were interested in racing, and in 1929, he founded Scuderia (meaning "stables", an Italian euphemism for a racing "team") Ferrari.

"The idea of the Scuderia first came up at a dinner party in Bologna in 1929 and was launched right away," wrote Ferrari. Scuderia, or team, Ferrari, lasted nine years and established Enzo Ferrari as the racing arm of Alfa Romeo. During the 1930s, Alfa Romeo cars prepared and entered by Scuderia Ferrari were very successful in sports car racing and Grand Prix events.

Enzo Ferrari was not an engineer, despite honorary engineering degrees accorded him later in life. He had no formal training of any kind. Nor was Ferrari a designer, a great mechanic, or champion race car driver. He was however, a determined visionary who could assemble a team of talented men and women to achieve the goals he set. In his own words, Enzo Ferrari was an "agitator of men." In 1939, Ferrari and Alfa Romeo parted ways, and in 1940, Ferrari built his first car, a Fiat-based race car called the Type 815. Ferrari, under terms set with Alfa Romeo, could not use his own name on a car for five years.

Using his skills as a machine shop operator, Ferrari survived the war by obtaining contracts from government agencies, and building various types of grinding machines. Although his shops were bombed during the war, Ferrari managed well and at the end of the conflict, he was ready to begin again, this time with his name on his own race car.

1945-1970: The Golden Era
Although this book deals with the V-8 Ferrari produced from 1976 to 1985, so much of the Ferrari legend and myth stems from the 12-cylinder cars, so they are worth addressing in some detail.

The inspiration for Ferrari's original V-12 came from an American car company. In the early 1900s, the Packard car company produced a series of highly successful four and six-cylinder luxury cars. In 1915 Packard introduced the world's first series production V-12, called the Twin Six. Many of these were used by

American Army officers in Europe during and after WWI, and Enzo Ferrari had been very impressed by the Twin Six engine. Ferrari's friend, race driver Antonio Ascari, purchased a racing version, which he later sold to another friend of Ferrari's, Baroness Maria Antonietta Avanzo. When he was ready to build a car of his own, Enzo Ferrari knew exactly what he wanted.

In July of 1945, with the war in Italy all but over, Enzo Ferrari placed a call to his longtime friend and associate, engineer Gioachino Colombo, who drew the plans for the first Ferrari, the 125S. The model name was derived from the fact that each cylinder had a total displacement of 125 cc. Thus, the first V12 was only 1500cc, or 90 cubic inches. The aluminum heads were a unique design, consisting of a single overhead camshaft on each bank, operating two valves per cylinder. The block was also aluminum, with cast iron liners.

On May 11th, 1947, the 125S, virtually identical to Colombo's drawings, made its debut at a small race in Piacenza, Italy. Two cars were entered, one withdrawn, the other retired. It was, according to Ferrari, "a promising failure." But during the next three months, the 125S Ferraris took part in ten more races, winning six. The firm from Maranello never looked back.

Ferrari next entered the world of Formula One racing. On September 5th, 1948, three F1 Ferraris entered the Italian Grand Prix. One finished in third place. It was the beginning of a glorious era for Ferrari.

Ferrari's primary goal was building a successful Grand Prix, or Formula One car. In 1950, the FIA created the World Driver's Championship, based on points won in a series of Grand Prix races. In general, each major European country was entitled to one Grand Prix that counted toward the Driver's Championship. (In the US, the Indianapolis 500 also counted for points, but was widely ignored by most European teams.)

After a season of using a supercharged 1500cc V-12 for his Formula 1 cars, Ferrari found it necessary to also build a larger displacement V-12 engine. Colombo, however, was now back at Alfa Romeo. Ferrari hired Aurelio Lampredi to design a 4.5 liter version of Colombo's small V12. The two engines were dubbed the "Colombo" and 'Lampredi" V12s, adding a bit of confusion to the Ferrari V-12 legend. The large block 4.5 liter engines powered the Grand Prix Ferraris of 1950-51, while the smaller "Columbo" engine powered the 166, 212, and 250 series sports cars.

For 1952, Formula One cars would be limited to 2 liters. Ferrari decided upon a dual overhead cam (DOHC) four cylinder engine rather than the V-12. With this new four cylinder, Ferrari won its first World Championship in 1952, with Alberto

Ascari driving. Ascari won again in 1953, and Ferrari drivers also won the Championship in 1956, 1958, 1961 and 1964.

As racing successes increased, so did the demand for the road cars. Ferrari was forced to pay more attention to the production of the various street Ferraris. Sales of the street cars enabled Ferrari to continue racing. In 1947, three road cars were produced; in 1950 the number rose to 26, and by 1960, Ferrari was producing 300-400 cars every year.

In the mid-1950s, a new class of sports cars, called "Grand Touring" became popular and the street cars once ignored by Ferrari became the prime weapon in the GT classes. Out of this grew the immortal GTO, or Gran Turismo Omologato. It was as if, for two golden decades between 1947 and 1967, everything the man from Maranello touched turned to gold. The Ferrari legend was born of these years.

Concurrent with the racing success of the V12 Ferrari, a group of Italian coachbuilders were creating breathtaking new automobile designs and building them individually, usually out of aluminum. Firms such as Vignale, Touring, Pininfarina, and Zagato competed with each other to create the finest, most beautiful bodies to adorn Ferrari chassis. The combination of the Ferrari chassis and the hand built creations of Italian coachbuilders electrified the world. Ferrari road cars were in demand by royalty, captains of industry and movie stars.

Although there have been many more victories since that era, royalty, CEOs, and rock stars still buy Ferraris (on a whim, Rod Stewart recently purchased a new Enzo, the top of the line Ferrari supercar), the first twenty years of Ferrari were the most glamorous, exciting, and enduring. The V12 legend and mystique were made during those years, never to be undone.

Ironically, Ferrari's V12s rarely won a Formula 1 race - information worth remembering as a Ferrari V-8 enthusiast. After the first successes in Formula 1 in 1951 with a 4.5 liter V-12, Ferrari Formula 1 cars were powered as follows:

1952-3	Ferrari 500	4 cylinder DOHC 2-liter
1954-5	Ferrari 625	4 cylinder DOHC, 2.5-liters
1955-57	Ferrari-Lancia D50	V-8, 2.5-liters
1958-60	246 Dino F1	V-6, 2.5-liters
1961-63	Dino 156	V-6, 1.5-liters
1964	158 F1	V-8, 1.5-liters
1965	512 F1	Flat 12, 1.5-liters
1966-69	312 F1	V12, 3-liters
1970-80	312 series	Flat 12, 3-liters
1981-88	Various models	V-6, 1.5-liters Turbocharged
1989-95	Various models	V-12, 3.5-liters
1996-05	Various models	V-10, 3-liters

After 55 years of Grand Prix Formula 1 racing, Ferraris powered by V-12 configurations won only 14 events.

Nevertheless, the V-12, in both big block "Lampredi" and small block "Colombo" forms, were dominant in sports car racing until the late 1960s. The immortal 250GT series, which produced the Tour de France, the Short Wheelbase Berlinetta, and the GTO, were three liter V-12s. The V-12 legend, though perhaps perverted, was deserved. Ferraris won the 1000 mile road race in Italy, appropriately called the "Mille Miglia" eight times from 1948 to 1957. Ferraris won at Le Mans nine times from 1948 to 1965. Almost all major Ferrari sportscar victories were achieved in V-12 engined cars, although there were many minor races won in four cylinder and six cylinder Ferraris, and the horizontally opposed (flat) 12 cylinder 312 P was successfully raced in the 1970s.

Throughout it all, Enzo Ferrari devoted his entire life to improving his cars; in essence, he had no personal life. His marriage to Laura Garello, at first happy, became strained, particularly after the tragic and untimely death of his only son Alfredino ("Dino" in the diminutive) in 1956. A long time affair with his mistress, Lina Lardi produced a son, Piero Lardi Ferrari, in 1945, an affair that was kept quiet for many years. Today, Piero Lardi is the titular head of Ferrari and the largest individual stockholder.

Despite the great successes of both his road and race cars, racing proved to be increasingly costly. By 1962 Ferrari was contemplating selling some or all of his company, of which he and his family owned 100%. In May of 1963, negotiations with Ford Motor Company began in detail. Ford agreed to pay Ferrari $18 million for 90 percent of the business. Ferrari would continue to be in charge of the racing department while the production of street cars would be the responsibility of Ford. The company would be renamed "Ford-Ferrari." The deal fell through when Ferrari realized he would not have complete, autonomous, control over the race program.

Ferrari's refusal to sell out to Ford launched the years of Ford racing, a hugely expensive program which saw the Ford GT 40s win at Le Mans from 1966 to 1969. The Ferrari-Ford battles proved expensive for Ferrari as well, and it showed. In the years 1967 to 1969, Ferrari won only one Formula 1 race.

As early as 1967, Ferrari was in contact with Gianni Agnelli of Fiat concerning the sale of Ferrari. On June 21st, 1969 the announcement was made. For $11 million, Fiat would purchase 40 percent of the Ferrari stock.

49 percent was to be left to Enzo Ferrari, 1 percent to Pininfarina, and the remaining 10 percent to Piero Lardi Ferrari. Fiat would take total control of the production cars, and leave Enzo Ferrari in total control of the race business. Upon Ferrari's death, Fiat would receive his 49 percent share, and become the largest shareholder. Until his death, however, Enzo Ferrari would have total control of his race cars and race teams.

1970-1988: A Changing World
By 1970, the world around Ferrari was changing rapidly. Thanks to the Fiat stock purchase, Ferrari survived. But everything was different.

The once-famous coachbuilding firms were failing, unable to keep pace with more modern technologies. Pininfarina, who adopted the latest mass manufacturing techniques, survived as the only major Italian coachbuilder. Virtually all Ferraris have been bodied by Pininfarina since 1954.

From the late 1960s through the 1970s, strikes and labor unrest at the Ferrari factory and throughout Italy caused loss of production, falling profits and general dismay in the industry. The oil crisis of 1973-4 and again in 1979 almost destroyed the entire supercar industry. At the same time, the U.S. government was instituting emissions and safety regulations that most car manufacturers found difficult and expensive to meet.

Ferrari found success with the 312P sports racer, which won the Manufacturers

Championship in 1972. In 1973, Ferrari decided to forgo sports, GT, and prototype racing to focus entirely on Formula 1. After an eleven year wait, Niki Lauda finally won the World Championship again in 1975. Lauda did it again in 1977 and Ferrari won again in 1979 with Jody Schecter.

Despite the social, political, and energy problems, Ferraris were succeeding in the marketplace. When Fiat took over the production of the road vehicles in 1969, the total number of road Ferraris built that year was only 619. By 1976, with the 308 series in production, the total per year had increased to 1426 automobiles. When Enzo Ferrari died in 1988, production had increased to over 4000 cars a year.

The Ferrari 365GTB/4, better known as the Daytona and introduced in 1968, was the last road going Ferrari built and designed under the direct control and supervision of Enzo Ferrari. Yet, remarkably, the Ferraris produced under Fiat control were, and continue to be, true Ferraris, a paradox which has no easy explanation. Let's just say it could only have happened that way in Italy. Most certainly this would not be the case had Ford bought Ferrari a few years earlier.

When the new "Dino", the 308GTB4, appeared in 1974, (bodied by Bertone, it would be the last Ferrari body to be built by any other firm aside from Pininfarina) plans were already afoot for it's replacement, the 308GTB and GTS. The 308 series cars were wildly successful. The 308GT was replaced by the improved 328GTB/S in 1986, and the Mondial series was launched in 1980 amid reservations but good sales.

In addition to the 308 series, the 365GT 2+2, 400GT, and 412 GT, originally introduced in 1972, were refined, four passenger Ferraris, much underrated then and still today. In 1973, the 365 GT/4, known as the Berlinetta Boxer became the first rear engined 12 cylinder car. This was followed by the Testarossa in 1984, which used the same engine in a new chassis and body. Testarossa means "Red Head" in Italian and refers to the color of the cam covers - it was an homage to the 1956-61 Testa Rossas. Also in 1984, the turbo V-8 powered 288 GTO became an instant classic, until the introduction of the F40 in 1987.

The 1980s saw a significant number of Ferrari victories in Formula One, including the Constructor's Title in 1982 and 1983. But despite the efforts of drivers such as Carlos Reuteman, Gilles Velleneuve, Didier Pironi, Rene Arnoux and Gerhard Berger, Ferrari would fail to capture the Driver's World Championship. But they never stopped trying.

On August 14th 1988, Enzo Ferrari, passed away. Along with him went an era of great racing and great cars.

1990-Present: The Fiat Era

The passing of Enzo Ferrari did nothing to slow the forward motion of technology, sales, and racing victories. Even more money was put into the Formula One program, more street cars were introduced, and production reached new highs. In the background, classic Ferraris were fetching huge prices and for a while, it looked like there was no limit to the insane prices being paid for any Ferrari. The bubble burst in 1991, and today, the market for used and classic Ferraris is fairly stable, and quite strong.

A new Chairman was appointed, Luca Montezemolo, who managed the racing team during the victorious Lauda years in the mid 1970s. It was not the Ferrari of old; instead, Ferrari faced the future with new ideas, new strategies, and above all, boldness. Ferrari aggressively licensed and marketed their name, logos, images, and the monies from these activities became a significant part of the company's revenue.

A new rear engine V-8 Ferrari, the 348, replaced the 328 series in 1990, and was in turn replaced by the five valve 355 in 1995. High tech solutions now meant more horsepower per liter, while exceeding the latest emissions and safety requirements. In 1992 a new V-12 appeared in the 465GT, with 5.5 liters producing 442 hp. In 1995 the top of the line was represented by the F50 Ferrari, to some degree a road going Formula One car with spectacular performance and a price tag to match.

For a brief time, Ferrari produced a sports racer, the 333 SP. But the factory did not race the cars. This was left to the private teams. On the Formula One front, a new V10 Ferrari was developed, and German driver Michael Schumacher was brought in to be the number one driver. Frenchman Jean Todt became the race manager and Englishman Rory Byrne headed the design team while Ross Brawn became the Chief Engineer. The team, once totally Italian, became a combination of talent from around the world.

The team effort brought four consecutive Driver's World Championships for Michael Schumacher, from 2000 to 2004, and becoming a six time World Champion, surpassing Juan Fangio's five driver's championships. Ferrari became the most successful manufacturer in Grand Prix racing.

Ferrari continued to develop and produce exciting, state of the art, new cars. The 360 Modena replaced the 355 in 1999, a completely new car that kept the paddle switch automatic gearbox technology developed on the 355. In 2005, the successor to the 360 came in the guise of the 430, still a rear-engine V-8, which traces its heritage directly back to the 308 series.

On the V-12 side of the house, the 550 Maranello was introduced in 1996, a GT coupe based on the 456 and superseded by the 575 M and the SuperAmerica. In 2004, the 612 Scaglietti was introduced.

Top of the line, at least for a while, was the F50 successor called the Enzo, in 2002. Production was discontinued in 2003 after 399 were produced.

In the late 1990s, a strange phenomenon occurred. Fiat, who had purchased the ailing firm of Maserati, decided to create a "bread and butter car" with the famous name, one which could compete with the upscale BMW, Lexus and Mercedes products. The Maserati product, a front engine, rear drive car with a Ferrari based V-8, was developed. Maserati became part of Ferrari and would be sold at all Ferrari dealerships.

As great as the early Maseratis were, Enzo Ferrari treated them as mortal enemies. His dislike of Maserati cars knew no bounds. Ironically, as if being condemned from the grave, the Ferrari-Maserati deal failed to work for Fiat. As of this writing, Maserati, a company still in debt, was transferred from Ferrari ownership to that of Alfa Romeo, another Fiat-owned company. This action could pave the way for an eventual Initial Public Offering for Ferrari itself.

Ferrari's Champion Drivers

1952, 1953	Alberto Ascari
1956	Juan Manual Fangio
1958	Mike Hawthorn
1961	Phil Hill
1964	John Surtees
1975, 1977	Niki Lauda
1979	Jody Scheckter
2000-04	Michael Schumacher

HISTORY OF THE 308

The development that led up to the 308 series spans 10 years, from the 1963 F1 engine and the first Dino 206 show car in 1965, to the first 308 GT4 in 1974. After that, the 308 series lasted the 11 years from 1974 to 1985.

The following timeline describes the history of the 308 series, starting with the Dino 206.

1957	The first Dino engine is made. It is a 65 degree V6.
1965	The Dino 206 show car is introduced at the Turin Show.
1966	The second Dino 206 prototype is introduced at the Turin Show.
1968	The Dino 206GT becomes available to customers. The engine is a 2 liter 65 degree V6 with a body designed by Pininfarina and built by Scaglietti.
1969	Just over 150 206GT's are made in 18 months.
1969	The 246 GT is introduced at the Geneva Motor Show. The engine is a 2419cc DOHC engine with 3 Weber 40 DCF carburetors.
1972	The Dino 246GTS is introduced at the Geneva Motor Show. The body is similar to the GT, but the roof is removable.
1974	In May, production of the Dino 246GT and 246GTS is stopped.
1974	The Dino 308GT4 is introduced with a body designed by Bertone. The engine is a 2926cc 90 degree V8.
1975	The Dino 308GT4 is introduced for the Italian market at the Geneva Motor Show.
1975	The Ferrari 308GTB is introduced at the Paris Motor Show. Pininfarina designed the fiberglass body. The Engine is the same but uses 3 Weber 40DCNF carburetors.
1977	In June the body manufacturing for the 308GTB changes to steel, after producing just 712 in fiberglass.
1977	The Ferrari 308GTS is introduced at the Frankfurt Motor Show.
1980	The Dino 308GT4 goes out of production. A total of 2826 are produced.
1980	Bosch K-Jetronic Fuel injection replaces the carburetors on the 308GTB and GTS for the 1981 model year. The designations are changed to GTBi and GTSi.
1982	In October, the Ferrari 308QV (Quattrovalvole) is introduced at the Paris Salon. There are now 4 valves per cylinder.
1985	Production of the 308QV is halted.

The 3 Liter V8

The Ferrari V-8 engine used in the 308 model series is derived from the 1.5 liter V-8 Formula One Grand Prix engine used by John Surtees to win the 1964 World Championship. The F1 engine was designed in 1963 by Angelo Bellei. Even though it did so well in competition, the V-8 design wasn't used in a road car until nearly ten years later, in the 308GT4.

One of the unique design choices in the engine was the use of a 180 degree crankshaft - basically a flat crankshaft with the throws and counterweights on either side. Ferrari has used five main bearing 180 degree crankshafts in nearly all of its 8 cylinder engines. This unique feature is part of what gives the engine such a distinctive exhaust sound.

The engine's total displacement was 2926cc (2.926 liters, or to put in U.S. measurements, 178.5 cubic inches). This value comes from a bore and stroke of 81mm and 71mm respectively. The engine was cast in a light aluminum alloy to keep the weight to a minimum. To increase the strength and durability of the cylinders, they were lined with nickel alloy inserts.

Throughout its production run, Ferrari's three liter engine went through several revisions and upgrades.

The engine of the 308GT4 started as a wet-sump oil system and was designated as F106AL. When the 308GTB was released the oil system was changed to a dry-sump, and the designation was changed to F106AB. When the final version was released for the Quattrovalvole, including increasing the number of valves, the designation changed to F105A.

Engine	Size	HP	Vehicle
F106AL	2926cc	205-250bhp	308GT4
F106C	1991cc	180bhp	208GT4
F106AB	2926cc	205-255bhp	308GTB/S carb.
F106BB	2926cc	205-214bhp	308GTBi/Si
DFE179V6G4V6		230-240bhp	308GTB/S QV in '83
EFE179V6F4V4		230-240bhp	308GTB/S QV after '83

Websites

- The FerrariList - http://www.FerrariList.com The FerrariList was formed in 1995 and has been growing ever since.

- Ferrari North America - http://www.FerrariUSA.com The official website of Ferrari North America.

- Ferrari S.p.A. - http://www.Ferrari.com The official Ferrari website based in Italy. There is also an English version.

- FerrariChat - http://www.FerrariChat.com This online Ferrari forum is based on a "Message Board" system, where topics are discussed via a useful web interface.

- Pininfarina - http://www.Pininfarina.it The official website of Pininfarina. Pininfarina is responsible for most of the Ferrari body designs.

- Shell-Ferrari Formula 1 - http://www.shellmotorsport.com/ferrari/. The official site of the Formula One Team Sponsor.

Books

- Original Ferrari V8: Restoration Guide for All Models by Keith Bluemel. This is the bible for 308's. There is no better book on 308 details. ISBN: 1870979788.

- Ferrari 1947-1997 by Antonio Ghini (Editor). Rizzoli International Publications; ISBN: 0847821528.

- Ferrari by Hartmut Lehbrink & Rainer W. Schlegelmilch. Konemann; ASIN: 3895080764. An excellent book, with excellent photography by Rainer Schlegelmilch.

- Ferrari: The Road Cars by Keith Bluemel. Sutton Publishing; ASIN: 0750919191. Keith Bluemel is one of the most knowledgeable Ferraristi in the world. His books are highly recommended.

- 50 Years of Ferrari: 1947-1997 by Andrea Curami (Editor) and Tony Antonini (Editor). Motorbooks International; ISBN: 0760304548.

- The Complete Ferrari by Roger Hicks. Motorbooks International; ASIN: 0760308071.

- Ferrari: The Legend on the Road by Brian Laban. Book Sales; ISBN: 0785812229.

CHAPTER 3　　　*The Ferrari 308 Models*

Between 1974 and 1985, Ferrari produced seven variations of the 308, each with its own pros and cons. This chapter provides an overview of the cars, including their similarities and differences. You can use this chapter to help you decide if a 308 is the right car for you, and if so, which 308 best fits your needs and requirements.

308GT4 2+2

In 1973, Ferrari's model line-up consisted of the 246, the 365GT/4 BB and 365 Daytona. While all the cars were great, the 246 needed more power and a more aggressive look. Ferrari needed something to compete with offerings from their competitors - Maserati's Merak, Lamborghini's Urraco, and Porsche's 911 were all newer and more advanced when compared to the aging 246. The answer to the competition was a more powerful V-8 engined car, with a body designed by Bertone. Like the Dino 246, the GT4 officially started its production run as a "Dino" and not a Ferrari. It's official designation, due to it's three liter engine, 8 cylinders and 4 seats (2 front and 2 rear) is the 308GT4 2+2.

The Dino 308GT4 2+2, introduced at the Paris Salon in October of 1973, was the first new Ferrari produced under the Fiat management. It was never stated specifically why Bertone was chosen to design the body of their new three liter car. Ferrari had used Pininfarina for almost 23 years and their designs were classic, stylish, and fit the image Ferrari wanted. Apparently, Fiat was very pleased with Bertone's Fiat Dino coupe, and he won the contract based on his previous efforts.

Design of the 308GT4 was difficult for Bertone for a number of reasons. He was asked to make a four passenger touring car with a large interior while keeping the car mid-engined. and with only a slight increase in wheelbase compared to the Dino 246. It was a difficult list of requirements to fit into a single vehicle. Bertone was known for using straight lines instead of Pininfarina's well known and very

Photo by Tom Reynolds

well loved graceful curves. Bertone's styling staff produced one of the least "Ferrari-looking" Ferraris ever released. Though just about everyone in the press and media thought it was unbecoming at best, there were a few people that thought it was bold and different (which it was). In fact, Bertone drove his GT4 for years.

While many Ferraristi refer to the GT4 as "the ugliest Ferrari", due to its styling, it represents the most inexpensive entry into Ferrari ownership. The technology, power, and handling of the car were, and still are, impressive and enjoyable.

By 1975, after nearly 2 years on the market, the GT4 sales were low enough that Ferrari decided to claim the car as its own - in the hopes that calling it an "official Ferrari" would increase the sales and desirability. The name-change ploy didn't work, and sales picked up only slightly. A total of 2826 GT4's were built by the end of the production run in 1980.

Although there were a variety of minor updates and modifications during the six and a half years of GT4 production, there was only one set of changes worthy of dividing the GT4 production run. In 1975 the front grill was changed from a deep front grill to a full width front grill, all the badges were replaced with "Ferrari" badging at the factory, and various options became standard features. The earlier cars are commonly referred to as Series 1, while the updated cars are referred to as Series 2.

Pros and Cons

Although most people feel that the GT4 isn't the most beautiful car ever made, it does represent a great value, which is good in some respects and horrible in others. In addition to the normal factors that go into deciding whether or not to purchase a 308, there are also several additional pluses and minuses that should be considered when looking seriously at a GT4.

Inexpensive Purchase Price

The GT4 is the least expensive Ferrari around. This can mean picking up an excellent example in top condition for under $30,000, or a good condition and usable example for around $20,000. The downside is that because they're available at "affordable" prices, they were often purchased by people with minimal knowledge of taking care of Italian exotics. Many of them have been neglected and have big repair bills in their future. Unless you love this 308 model, you definitely don't want to own a "project" GT4.

Expensive Repair Costs

Although they don't look like most Ferraris, the GT4s command the same high price for parts and labor that other Ferraris require. They share many of the same mechanical parts as the GTB's and GTS's, but the body and most of the interior parts are completely different. And the most important factor - they're older than all the other 308s, meaning that they've had that much more time to deteriorate.

Unique Styling

Because of its unique styling, many bystanders don't even notice it, and fewer still are familiar with it or its heritage. This is a positive aspect if you don't want the attention that a "common" 308 brings, or if you're the unusual type that likes being different. If you're looking forward to seeing people's faces light up when you tell them it's a Ferrari, and would be disappointed with a response of "No, seriously, what kind of car is it?," a GT4 might not be for you.

Insurance and Purchase Loans

One might encounter problems in obtaining either financing for purchasing a GT4 and insuring it thereafter. The difficulty lies in the perceived value of the car.

Depending on what value tables you look at, you're buying a 30 year old car with debatable resale value. Most standard banks won't even touch a loan like that, and insurance companies are much the same way.

It's a Ferrari

The 308GT4 is a Ferrari. It's got all the mechanical components designed by Ferrari, and most importantly, it sounds like a Ferrari. It's got that Ferrari spirit running through its veins and you can feel it when you drive it. The spirit and soul are definitely there.

A Unique Ferrari

If you're one who likes to enjoy things from a completely different perspective, the GT4 may be the right choice. There are dedicated groups of fans and aficionados that love these cars. Like anything unique and different, it attracts groups of supporters that are often more enthusiastic and interested in helping fellow owners out. This camaraderie exists with all 308 owners, but the "GT4 crowd" is a very supportive sub-group.

"4" Seats

Yes, it does officially have 4 seats, but the only passengers that comfortably fit are either under ten years old, or have no legs. They can fit if it's an emergency, but it's best to think of it as a 2-seater with a big storage area behind the front seats.

308 GT4 Specifications

Engine:	Transverse, mid-mounted 90° V8, light alloy cylinder block and
Bore & Stroke:	81 x 71 mm
Displacement:	2,926.90 cc / 178.6 cu in
Compression	8.8:1
Max. Power	255 bhp @ 7,700 rpm; 85 bhp/liter
Timing Gear:	2 valves per cylinder, twin overhead camshafts per cylinder bank
Fuel System:	4 Weber 40 DCNF carburetors
Ignition:	Single plug, 2 coils
Transmission:	Dry single-plate clutch, 5-speed gearbox + reverse, ZF limited-slip
Chassis:	Tubular
Suspension:	Independent, double wishbones, coil springs
Brakes:	Discs, servo assist
Steering:	Rack and pinion
Cooling System:	1 front radiator
Wheelbase:	2,550mm
Front/ Rear Track:	1,470/1,460 mm
Dry Weight (US):	1,450 kg
Tires:	205-70 VR 14
Fuel Tank:	80 liters
Top Speed:	250 km/h

308GTB/GTS

The Ferrari 308GTB was introduced at the Paris Motor Show in 1975. When compared side-by-side to the GT4, even though the engine and drive train are nearly identical, the GTB is far sexier. The lines and curves of the GTB recalls memories of the 246 Dino.

This time the styling was done by Pininfarina, who had less stringent passenger requirements - the newest 8 cylinder would be a two-seater. The GTB's wheelbase was moved back to 92.1 inches (from 100.4in), the same as the 246's, while the height was dropped from 47.6 inches to 44.1 inches. The weight of the car was also down about 40 pounds.

Pininfarina's design was unique and impressive. The critics of the time were universally impressed with its flowing and aggressive curves. The design is now undeniably a classic. Its status in Ferrari's history is secure. In fact, when most people think of "Ferrari," the first image that pops into their head is that of the 308GTB or GTS.

The new body design was also constructed very differently. For the first time in its history, Ferrari used fiberglass for the body parts of one of its production cars. The quality of the fiberglass was very high, but after about a year Ferrari changed production to traditional steel body parts. Only 712 fiberglass cars were produced. Due to their rarity, lighter weight and rust-free bodies, they usually command the highest prices for any of the 308s.

In 1977 Ferrari introduced a "spider" version of the GTB, called the 308GTS, which had a removable fiberglass top. The targa top was extremely light, but the extra chassis reinforcements added over 60 pounds to the total weight of the car. The open version of the 308 quickly became the favorite, and Ferrari's production numbers show it - 4139 GTB's were made, while 8010 GTS's were made. Even though there were more GTS versions made, they still command a higher price in today's market.

The engine of the new 308 was nearly identical to the engine used in the GT4. The four Weber 40DCNF carburetors were still functioning great, as were the sounds they generated while sucking intake air from the passenger side air inlet.

Model Year Information

1975	Fiberglass body GTB introduced (First SN: 18677)
1976	Last Fiberglass body made (SN: 21289). 712 Fiberglass cars were made. First steel bodied GTB made (SN: 20805).
1977	First 308GTS made (SN: 22619).
1980	Last steel bodied 308GTB made. (SN: 34349) 2185 steel 308GTB's made. Last steel bodied 308GTS made (SN: 34501). 3219 steel bodied 308GTS's made.

EURO CARS

In the late 70's and early 80's, Ferrari, like many other European car manufacturers, produced two distinct versions of their cars. One produced for the increasing safety and emissions standards in the United States, and another produced for the relatively relaxed European standards. Vehicles destined for the US were hampered with a number of power sapping, weight increasing emission control "features."

Larger steel bumpers were mounted on the so called "US 308" with all the heavy supporting hardware adding over 200 pounds. Catalytic converters both weighed more and were more restrictive. Headers on the US cars were smaller and more restrictive. Emissions were met by slapping on an air pump which sapped nearly 20hp from the engine, while adding additional dead weight.

The European cars were rated at 255bhp, while the US cars were rated at 240bhp. This difference is quite noticeable, and explains why the imported "Euro" version 308's, with correct Department of Transportation (DOT) paperwork, typically sell for 2-5 thousand dollars more than their US counterparts.

Pros and Cons
There are several factors to reflect on when seriously considering the purchase of a "carbed" 308

Looks

The GTB and GTS cars are among the most breath-taking automobiles ever made. This has both positive and negative effects. It's great to drive and be seen in such a car, but also be prepared for stares, finger pointing, tail-gaters, and challenges from every street racer you see.

Carburetors

Carburetors sound great, there's no doubt about it. But, there is a reason they're not used anymore. They're touchy, inflexible in operation, difficult to set-up correctly, and time-consuming to maintain. You've got four individual carbs that must be adjusted and synchronized. It isn't extremely difficult if you have the right tools and training, but be prepared to spend time with your carbs. Mis-adjusted carbs can cause a variety of expensive damage to the engine, so paying attention to them is required if you want that beautiful intake sound.

"Slow Down Lights"

On US versions of the 308's equipped with catalytic converters, there are two lights on the bottom of the dash, on either side of the steering column, labeled "Slow Down cyl 1-4" and "Slow Down cyl 5-8". These lights will illuminate if the catalytic converters get too hot. And if they come on while you're driving, pull over immediately - they're serious. Euro cars, without catalytic converters do not have the slow-down lights.

Wheel Size

The standard wheels on the carbureted 308's were 14 inches in diameter. Although 14" wheels were an option on the injected cars, 15" were standard equipment on the later 308's. If you're planning on getting new wheels and rims anyway, this won't matter, but if you want to keep your 308 original, you'll have smaller wheels than the later models.

Ferrari 308GTB Euro Specifications

Engine:	Transverse, mid-mounted 90° V8, light alloy cylinder block and head.
Bore & Stroke:	81 x 71 mm
Displacement:	2,926.90 cc / 178.6 cu in
Compression Ratio:	8.8:1
Max. Power Output:	255 bhp @ 7,700 rpm; 85 bhp/liter
Timing Gear:	2 valves per cylinder, twin overhead camshafts per cylinder bank
Fuel System:	4 Weber 40 DCNF carburetors
Ignition:	Single plug, 2 coils
Transmission:	Dry single-plate clutch, 5-speed gearbox + reverse, ZF limited-slip differential
Chassis:	Tubular
Suspension:	Independent, double wishbones, coil springs
Brakes:	Ventilated discs
Steering:	Rack and pinion
Cooling System:	1 front radiator
Wheelbase:	2,340mm
Front/ Rear Track:	1,460/1,460 mm
Dry Weight:	1,330 kg
Tires:	205-70 VR 14
Fuel Tank:	Two 70-80 liter tanks
Top Speed:	252 km/h

308GTBI/GTSI

By 1979 it was apparent that the carbureted car couldn't continue to meet the increasingly aggressive US emissions standards. The "patch-work" of air-pumps, heat reducers and catalytic converters couldn't keep up with the tightening legal demands. Unfortunately, the state of fuel injection technology at Ferrari was limited and a solution was needed quickly. The new fuel injected four valve head was the answer but it wasn't ready yet.

In order to keep selling cars in the United States, Ferrari introduced a two valve per cylinder, fuel injected engine that used the K-Jetronic fuel injection system from Bosch. Though the power was down, they were able to meet standards and import the car into the United States - their biggest market.

The engine was designated F106BB, and produced a claimed 205bhp on the US version and 214bhp on the Euro version. This was a significant drop in power from the carbureted cars. Nearly a 30bhp loss, which is very noticeable when driving the early injected cars after driving an earlier carbureted car or a later Quattrovalvole. Ferrari produced the GTBi and GTSi cars for about two years, making 494 GTBi's and 1749 GTSi's. Their reduced power output makes their prices a great bargain, if the slower acceleration isn't an annoyance to you. Their prices typically fall between the GT4 on the low side and the carbureted cars on the higher side.

There were few interior or exterior changes throughout production of the 308 series. Interior changes for the injected cars included small changes such as changing the dash material from brushed aluminum in the early 308's to matte black on the injected models, as well as a different position for the clock and oil temperature gauge.

The exterior of the injected cars is nearly identical to that of the carburetor versions. There was now a single exhaust on the driver side as well as a small "i" included after the GTB/GTS plaques on the rear of the car and on the passenger side dashboard.

PROS AND CONS

Inexpensive
Of all the two-seater 308's, the injected models nearly always sell for less than a comparable carbureted or QV version. The reason of course is due to the 2 valve injected cars' lower power and torque.

Power
They are the "slowest" of the entire 308 series. If the decrease in power doesn't concern you, this may be the 308 for you. It's slower, but has all the look and most of the feel. Even the European version is limited in power.

Ferrari 308GTBi/GTSi Specifications

Engine:	Transverse, mid-mounted 90° V8, light alloy cylinder block and head.
Bore & Stroke:	81 x 71 mm
Displacement:	2,926.90 cc / 178.6 cu in
Compression Ratio:	8.8:1
Max. Power Output:	205 bhp @ 6,600 rpm; 71 bhp/liter
Timing Gear:	2 valves per cylinder, twin overhead camshafts per cylinder bank
Fuel System:	Bosch K-Jetronic Mechanical Injection
Ignition:	Single plug, 2 coils
Transmission:	Dry single-plate clutch, 5-speed gearbox + reverse, ZF limited-slip differential
Chassis:	Tubular
Suspension:	Independent, double wishbones, coil springs
Brakes:	Ventilated discs
Steering:	Rack and pinion
Cooling System:	1 front radiator
Wheelbase:	2,340mm
Front/ Rear Track:	1,460/1,460 mm
Dry Weight (US):	GTB: 1,447 kg / GTS: 1,465kg
Tires:	205-70 VR 14
Fuel Tank:	Two 70-80 liter tanks
Top Speed:	235 km/h

308GTBI/GTSI QUATTROVALVOLE

To resolve the limited horsepower problem of the injected version, while keeping the cleaner exhaust, in 1983 Ferrari introduced a four valve per cylinder 308. The additional intake and exhaust valves help the engine breath and generate more power.

There are actually two versions of the Quattrovalvole (most commonly called simply "QV"). The 1983 QV was simply a four valve head bolted onto the standard three liter engine, while the 84 and 85 QVs received updated emissions equipment, Nikasil cylinder liners, and a factory claimed five additional horsepower.

The body was only slightly modified from the injected 308. The most recognizable difference was the addition of a "center" grille on the front lid. The louvered area matched the louvers behind the headlights and provided hot air extraction from the front mounted radiator. All US cars had this area painted black, while the European cars were painted to match the body color.

The bumpers on the US cars, like all previous 308s, were a stronger and heavier version compared to the European version. They were also matte black and protruded further out than the European counterpart. In early 1984, Ferrari started adding additional rust protection to the QV.

QV Model Year Information

1982	The Quattrovalvole is introduced in October at the Paris Salon Auto Show.
1983	First production 308QV is made.
1985	Last 308QV is made. 1344 308QV GTB's made. 6068 308QV GTS's made.

PROS AND CONS

Power and Refinements

The power and refinements made to the QV make it the most updated 308 available. If you've decided on a 308, and price is not an issue, the QV is your best option. Power of the QV matches and, in most setups, exceeds the carbureted versions, even with the additional emission equipment installed. The fuel injection setup is clean and reliable, and ultra-simple to maintain when compared to the Weber carburetors.

Cost

The downside of the most recent 308 technology is the cost. QV sale prices can be 30% to 40% higher than other 308s, and sometimes double the price of a GT4. In some cases, the price for an excellent condition QV will be as much as a good condition early 328.

308 GTBi/GTSi QUATTROVALVOLE (US VERSION)

Engine:	Transverse, mid-mounted 90° V8, light alloy cylinder block and head. US: F105A/40 Euro: F105A (aka Tipo F105AB)
Bore & Stroke:	81 x 71 mm
Displacement:	2,926.90ci / 178.6cc
Compression	US: 9.2:1 Euro: 8.6:1
Max. Power	240 bhp @ 7,000 rpm; 85 bhp/liter
Timing Gear:	4 valves per cylinder, twin overhead camshafts per cylinder bank
Fuel System:	Bosch K-Jetronic mechanical injection
Ignition:	Single plug, Digiplex Marelli
Transmission:	Dry single-plate clutch, 5-speed gearbox + reverse, ZF limited-slip
Chassis:	Tubular
Suspension:	Independent, double wishbones, coil springs
Brakes:	Ventilated discs
Steering:	Rack and pinion
Cooling System:	1 front radiator

Wheelbase:	2,340 mm
Front/Rear Track:	1,460/1,460 mm
Dry Weight:	GTB: 1,447 kg / GTS: 1,465 kg
Tires:	240/55/VR15
Fuel Tank:	74 Liters in two tanks
Top Speed:	255 km/h

WHICH 308 FOR YOU?

Which Model

After learning about the different choices, which 308 is for you? Would the lower purchase price of a GT4 overcome its less-than-pedigree shape? Does the do-it-yourself nature of tuning your own carbs make the carbureted 308 sound like fun? Or does the higher power Quattrovalvole sound like a better choice and worth the increased cost? Is the lower power of a GTBi or GTSi an acceptable trade-off for the lower prices? Or, does it sound like a newer 8-cylinder Ferrari might be a better fit? If a 328, 348, or 355, is within your price range, does it make more sense to go with one of them instead?

Open or Closed Top?

First, you'll need to decide if you want a GTS or GTB. Does the open top cruising element sound like fun, or does the stiffer and lighter GTB sound more interesting.

GTB

The coupe features the pure, classic Pininfarina design, while the spider is more of an afterthought. In addition, the GTB chassis is connected and triangulated more efficiently, so the chassis has less flex than an open-top GTS. The GTB is also lighter, because of the additional stabilization installed in the GTS. Safety is the other benefit of having a closed top. Finally, fewer GTBs were produced than GTSs.

GTS

Many Ferrari drivers prefer the open-air driving that a GTS provides. The adage, if the top goes down, the price goes up applies here. If you are a tall driver (over 6'2"), it may be more comfortable to always drive with the top off. In addition, a GTS with the top off is much easier to get into and out of.

Euro Version vs. US

On a level playing field, the Euro versions are almost always better. As produced for the European market, they weigh less and they have more power. However, when brought to the U.S. and legalized, that Euro version may suffer the same fate as the dealer-sold U.S. version, and still not meet emissions and safety standards. The front area below the bumper is also more aggressive looking and more desirable. They can be harder to locate and, if you find one, make sure that it has all the proper papers.

Condition

In nearly all cases, buying the best car in your price range is the best advice. But have a reasonable price range in mind. Right now $30k would buy an excellent condition GTBi with full records, while the same amount would get you a lower end QV that probably needs work. You've got to weigh your budget accordingly.

MORE INFORMATION

Websites

* The 308 FAQ - http://home.att.net/~ferrari/ Started and maintained by long-time Ferrari-lister Hunter N. Schultz, this is the list of frequently asked questions (with answers) for 308 owners. The site includes DIY instructions for many of the procedures the owner/mechanic might want to do.
* Ferrari308.com - http://www.ferrari308.com/ The Ferrari308 is a great small site with enough information to get you started in many aspects of Ferrari 308 ownership.
* 308GTB Registry - http://www.r-design.net/308/ Owner registry for owners of carbureted 308GTBs.
* 208/308GT4 Registry - http://www.dino-gt4-registry.com/ Owner registry for owners of Dino/Ferrari 208 and 308GT4s.
* 308QV Registry - http://www.308qvregister.com/ Owner registry for owners of 308 Quatrovalvoles.

Books

* Original Ferrari V8 by Keith Bluemel. Motorbooks International; ISBN: 1870979788. One of the best Ferrari books you could ever purchase. It contains just about everything you'd ever need to know about a V8 Ferrari. It has many lists and descriptions of the options and specifications of the V8 family. If you're going to buy a 308, you must have this book.
* The Ferrari Dino 246, 308 and 328 Collector's Guide by Alan Henry. Motorbooks International; ASIN: 0947981233.
* Complete Guide to Ferrari 308 Series by Wallace Wyss. Motorbooks International; ISBN: 0901564583.

308 Series Comparison Chart

	GT4	GTB/GTS	GTBi/GTSi	QV GTB/GTS
Engine Size	2926cc/ 178.5ci			
Bore & Stroke	81mm x 71 mm			
Valves	16	16	16	32
Fuel Delivery	Carbs	Carbs	Fuel Injection	Fuel Injection
Compression	8.8:1	8.8:1	8.8:1	8.6:1

308 Production Quantities

308 Model	Quantities	Serial Range
GT4	2826	07202 - 15604
GTB - Fiberglass	712	18677 - 21289
GTB - Steel	2185	20805 - 34349
GTS	3219	22619 - 34501
GTBi	494	31327 - 43059
GTSi	1749	31309 - 43059
GTBi QV	748	42809 - 59071
GTSi QV	3042	41701 - 59265

CHAPTER 4   *The Search*

So, you've decided on which 308 model you want and you've started looking for the perfect match. The search for a 308 is often long and time-consuming, but it's worth the wait. By putting some time and effort into the search, your ownership can be filled with a lot of fun and thrilling driving and a lot less time in the repair shop.

FINDING THE RIGHT 308

Buying a Ferrari isn't like going out and buying a standard American or Japanese import. Even though the price of your 308 is going to be similar to new large SUV's, the car is nevertheless an exotic. If the previous owner didn't take care of the car, you're going to pay for their laziness. Buying the right Ferrari can reap all sorts of benefits, while buying the wrong 308 could make ownership unbearable.

Before Starting
Once you've decided that you really want a 308, you'll need to decide what kind (GT4, GTB, GTS, etc.). Next, you'll need to decide what colors (interior and exterior), and what options you'll need.

To help you narrow your decisions, you should sit down and think about how you're really going to use the car. If you're going to show the car, the appearance is going to factor heavily. But, if you plan on racing your 308, the outward appearance isn't going to matter nearly as much. If you're a mechanic at heart, and have more time than money, a fixer-upper just might be for you. Just make sure you know how much the replacement parts are going to cost before you buy a "Ferrari-in-Need".

Be aware that you shouldn't fall in love with the first car that you find. Even if it is perfect, you should find at least one other possible car that you could buy. This helps for a couple of reasons. First, it gives you something to compare against, and second, it gives you a bargaining tool when negotiating the sale price of the car that you really want.

SELLERS

There are any number of reasons that a 308 can be for sale. The most common is that it's a dealership, and it's their job to sell cars. For private sellers, the reasons are almost always different, but it comes down to one thing for all of them: how much money can I get for this Ferrari?

Authorized Dealers
Ferrari North America (the North American division of Ferrari SpA) oversees all authorized Ferrari dealers. As of this writing there are 28 authorized dealers in North America. Ferrari North America (FNA) is based in New Jersey and oversees all aspects of new Ferrari sales in North America. They also track the used vehicle sales at their authorized dealerships. They help the "home office" in Italy evaluate the North American market, and make sure North America gets its fair share of new automobiles.

If you're looking for the "safest" place to get your 308, an authorized dealer is your best choice. This is true for a number of reasons. They have the most trained and knowledgeable technicians and mechanics for your 308 (though most of their training may be in the newer models). They will be able to perform the most thorough check and updates on all used vehicles they have in inventory. They have a responsibility to FNA to make sure they don't sell sub-par vehicles (FNA checks on customer satisfaction from all of its authorized dealers). Authorized dealers can also offer limited warranties on used vehicles they sell. Unfortunately, as the 308 series gets older, Ferrari dealers are less and less inclined to stock and sell them.

That being said, an authorized Ferrari dealer is a car dealer first and can make mistakes, sell faulty vehicles, fail to honor warranties, etc. Do not, for any reason, believe that an authorized Ferrari dealer is the closest thing to perfect.

The dealers currently authorized by Ferrari North America are:

Algar Ferrari of Philadelphia
1234 Lancaster Avenue
P.O. Box 167
Rosemont, PA 19010
(610) 527-1100
(610) 525-0575

The Auto Gallery
24050 Ventura Blvd.
Calabasas, CA 91302
(818) 884-4411
(818) 591-5894

Cauley Ferrari Maserati
7070 Orchard Lake Road
West Bloomfield, MI 48322
(248) 538-9600
(248) 538-9601

The Collection
200 Bird Road
Coral Gables, FL 33146
(305) 444-5555
(305) 444-8237

Continental Auto Sports
420 East Ogden Avenue
Hinsdale, IL 60521
(630) 655-3535
(630) 655-3541

Ferrari of Atlanta
11875 Alpharetta Highway
Roswell, GA 30076
(678) 802-5000
(678) 802-5019

Ferrari Beverly Hills
9372 Wilshire Blvd
Beverly Hills, CA 90212
(310) 275-4400
(310) 246-0400

Ferrari of Central Florida
525 South Lake Destiny Drive
Orlando, FL 32810
(407) 667-4300
(407) 667-4301

Ferrari of Central New Jersey
816 Route 1 North
Edison, NJ 08817
(732) 248-9100
(732) 248-9220

Ferrari of Cincinnati
429 Ohio Pike
Cincinnati, OH 45255
(800) 407-3832

Ferrari of Cleveland
99 Broadway Avenue
Bedford, OH 44146
(440) 359-1520

Ferrari of Dallas - Boardwalk Ferrari
6300 International Parkway
Plano, TX 75093
(972) 447-5200
(972) 447-5225

Ferrari of Denver
1480 East County Line Road
Highlands Ranch, CO 80126
(303) 730-7340
(303) 797-8874

Ferrari of Hawaii
1069 S. Beretania Street
Honolulu, HI 96814
(808) 585-6602
(808) 585-6611

Ferrari of Houston
6100 Southwest Freeway
Houston, TX 77057
(713) 772-3868
(713) 772-1472

Dealers currently authorized by Ferrari North America *(continued):*

Ferrari of Long Island
112 Glen Street
Glen Cove, NY 11542
(516) 671-7575
(516) 671-0569

Ferrari of Minneapolis
13708 Wayzata Blvd.
Minnetonka, MN 55305
(952) 797-1777

Ferrari of New England
1203 Washington Street
West Newton, MA 02465
(617) 559-0123
(617) 559-0075

Ferrari of Newport Beach
1000 West Coast Highway
Newport Beach, CA 92663
(949) 646-6900
(949) 646-7037

Ferrari of Ontario
5243 Steeles Avenue West
Toronto, Ontario M9L 2W2
Canada
(416) 749-5325
(416) 749-7675

Ferrari of Orange County
1425 West Baker Street
Costa Mesa, CA 92626
(714) 662-7600
(714) 662-7555

Ferrari of Pasadena
300 South Fair Oaks Ave
Pasadena, CA 91105
(800) 490-4145

Ferrari of Quebec
5155 de Sorel
Montreal, Quebec H4P 1G7
(514) 337-7274
(514) 340-9188

Ferrari of Rancho Mirage
71-387 Highway 111
Rancho Mirage, CA 92270
(800) 347-4709

Ferrari of San Antonio
15423 IH 10 West
San Antonio, TX 78249
(210) 341-2800
(210) 341-5260

Ferrari of San Diego
7477 Girard Avenue
La Jolla, CA 92037
(858) 454-9211
(858) 454-9227

Ferrari of San Francisco
595 Redwood Highway
Mill Valley, CA 94941
(415) 380-9700
(415) 380-0365

Ferrari of Seattle
1401 12th Avenue
Seattle, WA 98122
(206) 329-7070
(206) 329-7073

Ferrari of St. Louis
One Arnage Blvd.
Chesterfield, MO 63005
(636) 449-0000

Ferrari of Silicon Valley
2750 El Camino Real
Redwood City, CA 94061
(650) 261-6000
(650) 361-9681

Ferrari of Tampa
11333 N. Florida Ave
Tampa, FL 33612
(813) 933-2811

Ferrari of Toronto
101 Avenue Road
Toronto, Ontario M5R 2G3
Canada
(416) 962-5325
(416) 962-5704

Ferrari of Vancouver
1290 Venables Street
Vancouver V6A 4B4
(604) 215-8778
(604) 215-0600

Ferrari of Washington
45235 Towlern Place
Sterling, VA 20166
(703) 478-3606
(703) 478-3769

Foreign Cars Italia
5603 Roanne Way
Greensboro, NC 27409
(336) 294-0200
(336) 294-9109

Foreign Cars Italia of Charlotte
5216 E. Independence Blvd.
Charlotte, NC 28212
(704) 535-7100

F.C. Kerbeck Ferrari
100 Route 73 North
Palmyra, NJ 08065
(856) 829-8200

Lake Forest Sportscars
990 North Shore Drive
Lake Bluff, IL 60044
(847) 295-6560
(847) 295-0965

Midwestern Auto Group
6335 Perimeter Loop Rd.
Dublin, OH 43017
(614) 889-2571
(614) 889-2877

Miller Motorcars
342 West Putnam Avenue
Greenwich, CT 06830
(203) 629-3890
(203) 629-1621

Park Place Ferrari
5300 Lemmon Avenue
Dallas, TX 75209
(214) 443-5215

Penske Wynn Ferrari
3131 Las Vegas Blvd South
Las Vegas, NV 89109
(702) 770-2000
(702) 770-2005

Ron Tonkin Gran Turismo
203 NE 122nd Avenue
Portland, OR 97230
(503) 255-7560
(503) 257-2407

Scottsdale Ferrari
6825 E. McDowell Road
Scottsdale, AZ 85257
(480) 991-5322
(480) 421-3805

Shelton Ferrari
5750 North Federal Highway
Fort Lauderdale, FL 33308
(954) 493-5211
(954) 772-2653

Steve Harris Imports
808 South Main Street
Salt Lake City, UT 84101
(801) 521-0340
(801) 521-0673

Wide World of Cars
125 East Route 59
Spring Valley, NY 10977
(845) 425-2600
(845) 425-2816

Local Independent Dealers

Independent (or "non-authorized") dealers can be one of the best sources for vehicles. If you happen to have an exotic car dealership near you, this can be one of the best ways to find and buy a Ferrari. If you are fortunate enough to live by one, you can ask around to find out their reliability and customer satisfaction, as well as keep an eye out on their reputation. There are many such dealers, ranging from small, one-man operations to fully-staffed dealerships.

Doing research on the dealership is a must. First, search the Internet for information on the dealership and any possible unsatisfied customers. Are there pages devoted to describing the downsides of that particular dealership? Are there unhappy customers putting up websites? Remember that these may be isolated incidents, with only one point of view (the unhappy customer's), but there is usually some truth to them. Next, check the local Better Business Bureau (http://www.bbb.org) to see if there are any claims against the dealership.

Once you've determined that they're an upstanding dealership, and making the customer happy is their main concern, investigate further. Don't call them before you've done your research. The connotation "used car salesman" didn't come around for nothing. Your best defense is knowledge of the product and business.

Non-local Independent Dealers

If you pick up any national automotive classifieds magazine (Ferrari Market Letter, duPont Registry, Hemmings Motor News, etc.), you'll find many advertisements are from dealers around the country. These dealers may have the car you're looking for, but from a distance, it can be difficult to know for sure. You'll need to travel to see and drive the car in question, adding to the cost of the purchase.

Like other dealers, always be sure to research their reputation before checking their inventory. The additional problems with non-local dealers are shipping costs of the vehicle, and resolving any post-purchase issues.

Auctions

There are many types of auctions, including online auctions, standard automotive auctions, and impound auctions. Their greatest benefit is that you may be able to get a great price. The down-side of auctions is that the great price comes with quite a few risks. And often the price isn't that great either!

Most importantly, a majority of auctions don't allow (usually due to time restrictions) for a complete checkout of the automobile up for auction. Most of these cars won't come with documentation, so there's a good chance they weren't kept up. In addition, you will probably never get to know the seller, who may be full of useful information.

It's also important to remember that bids are almost always a legally binding contract, meaning, if you place a bid, and nobody bids more than you, you must complete the auction and pay the amount of your bid.

eBay

eBay is the world's largest online auction website, and it's also one of the most common auction locations to buy and sell Ferraris. There are so many vehicles sold through eBay, that they started a section devoted to them called eBay Motors (http://www.ebaymotors.com). There are usually several 308's up for auction at any one time on eBay.

The best way to search for a 308 on eBay is to search for "Ferrari 308." When you get the full listing of all items, click on the "Price" link at the top of the price column. This sorts the search results, with the highest priced items at the top. The full cars are usually listed first, followed by various parts and pieces.

The worst thing about bidding on vehicles up for auction on eBay (or any other internet auction site) is your inability to examine the car before you bid. Sure the descriptions tell all about the car, but there are no guarantees that the information in the description is accurate. In fact, if they include pictures of the car, it might not be the car you're bidding on! Unlike other auctions, where you have a chance to at least visually see (and hear) the car, this is not generally possible via eBay. There have been cases where the car failed to sell, and the potential buyer then visited the seller to see and inspect the car. But this is not the normal operating procedure for eBay sales.

Another thing to consider about Internet auctions is the payment method outlined in the auction. Some may put a deadline on the final payment date, as well as putting a very short (2-3 days) time limit for a down payment (usually 10 or 20 percent of the winning bid). Make sure to read the description and payment terms before bidding on anything.

Police and Government Auctions

It's a pretty safe bet that any Ferrari you find at a police or "confiscated" type auction won't be in good shape. There are rare exceptions, but not many. Keep that in mind when bidding. Unless you're an experienced mechanic and have a great source for replacement parts, I'd highly recommend not purchasing from a police or impound auction.

If you do decide to attend a government auction, you'll have to first find out where they're held, and what you'll need to attend. There are several web sites that specialize in police and seizure auctions, but most charge for the information. Occasionally, the listings for public auctions will appear in the classifieds or legal section of the local newspaper. You can also call your local government and simply ask.

Automotive Auctions
These are auctions like the famous Barret Jackson Auction in Arizona, which use the traditional auction technique.

There is a huge and updated list of automotive auctions in the Hemmings Motor News monthly magazine. There are also yearly and semi-annual auctions held specifically for rare and exotic cars. The prices for cars reached at these auctions tend to affect the rest of the market, since many dealers and brokers pay a lot of attention to what goes on at these auctions. Remember that the buyer is often responsible for commissions, and taxes may include local and state taxes, all in addition to the final hammer price. Suddenly, that good auction price may be more than what it seemed. Finally, you must get your new purchase home, adding the additional cost of transportation.

In summary, auctions are not the ideal marketplace for a first time Ferrari buyer. Leave auctions to those with a lot of experience.

Private Sellers
Ferrari owners eventually sell their cars, for a variety of reasons. Most owners of good 308's are sad to sell their Ferrari, but at least they can make someone else happy.

You can find plenty of private sellers in your local newspapers and national classified ads magazines (Ferrari Market Letter, Hemmings, duPont Registry, etc.). This is often the least expensive route, if price is the major factor. Remember, there is little or no recourse if you find problems after the sale.

Word of Mouth
Many Ferraris are sold simply by word of mouth, via local clubs or chat sites, car events or barbershops! This is often the best way to find a car. The previous owner is almost always an enthusiast, and wants to see the car go to another enthusiast. If you live in a large city, find the local Ferrari nuts and get the word out that you are in the market. Tell the local authorized or unauthorized dealers you are in the market-they may not be interested in dealing with an old Ferrari, but may pass sellers of such cars on to you.

Classifieds Ads

Check the local and national papers for classified ads. Smaller towns rarely have Ferraris listed in their ads, so if you live in a small town, check some of the larger cities' papers. You can usually find large city newspapers at bookstores, or find their classified ads section on the web.

Don't bother to call any ads that don't meet the specific type of 308 you're looking to purchase. If you find an ad that is worth calling, use the list of questions in the following section, and take ample notes. If, after the phone conversation, the car still looks interesting, schedule a time to view the car and take it for a test drive.

Ferrari Market Letter

The Ferrari Market Letter (known as FML in most Ferraristi circles) is a private publication published by long-time Ferraristi Gerald Roush. It's been publishing classified ads for Ferrari cars and assorted merchandise for nearly 30 years. Though not always just private sellers (there are a lot of dealers putting ads in), there are literally hundreds of Ferraris in the FML. They also have an online version available.

Subscriptions for the Ferrari Market Letter can seem a little steep (currently $40 for an online subscription and $100 for a print subscription for 6 months), but the information and ads can be invaluable in your search for a quality 308. If you don't find any immediate possible candidates, FML will definitely give you some leads. It's also helpful in determining the market asking prices for all types of Ferraris.

Hemmings Motor News

Hemmings Motor News is the thick dark yellow catalog-sized magazine you see at most periodical racks near the rest of the automotive magazines. Hemmings was started in 1954 and has grown to one of the largest and most widely read automotive classified ad publications. The magazine is published monthly, and lists a large variety of collectible and exotic cars. As you can imagine, it is packed with thousands of ads for the various makes and models. Like the Ferrari Market Letter, it also has a combination of private sellers and dealers.

Brokers

Because Ferraris are in relatively short supply, it is possible that you won't find exactly what you're looking to buy. When you think you need outside help in finding your 308, you can try using a broker or locating service. Brokers and locating services will search for a car matching your description. They do this by having a large network of contacts that have the ability to find cars matching your exact requirements.

But brokers don't work for free. They usually charge a small percentage of the sale price, or in some cases, a flat fee for finding a vehicle. You should only use a broker or locating service as a last resort though, because they can add a significant amount to the price. Also, most 308s are not in extremely short supply, so it's often best to look yourself for 5 or 6 months before hiring anyone to help. If you're going to use a broker or locating service to sell your car, only pay on the completed sale of the car.

GET THE FACTS

Once you have focused on a particular car, it's time to get very serious and make further inquiries.

Telephone Questions

Whatever the source, the first thing to do is interview the seller on the phone to see if this car is even close to what you want. You can save a lot of time and money by "pre-qualifying" a vehicle before you spend the time to visit or test drive the vehicle. Even if the car does not meet your qualifications, if the seller is nearby, you may still want to test drive it to get a feel for the types of cars available, and to give you a perspective on the model version you're looking at purchasing.

At the end of this chapter is a form and notes area to help guide you through the questions you'll want to ask.

Documentation

Documentation is all forms of paperwork related to the car. Things like original owners manual, factory service guides, registration information, smog check receipts, parts receipts, mechanic receipts, dealer receipts, insurance statements, and just about anything else. Although often overlooked, the documentation of a car can show a lot of "circumstantial" evidence that the car was taken care of. If documentation isn't present, it doesn't necessarily make a car bad, it just helps when it is there.

The most important piece of documentation is the title. There is no sense getting excited about a car which does not have a good, clean and very legitimate title. If it is a "salvage" title, it probably has had some serious damage in the past. Though this might not be the case for all cars, the high price of repair vs. the low cost of purchase can often make 308s a "salvaged" car with a small fender bender! If there is a lien against the car, it will often be marked on the back of the title. The title should have the correct VIN number, make, model, and year, as well as the current owner's correct name. Make sure the title is in good order.

CarFax

CarFax is one of the greatest inventions for the used car buyer. You can get all the previously reported insurance and state/federal data about the car, including accident claims, registration times (usually with mileage), emission test results and previous owners' information. Having this information is extremely useful in helping to determine if a car has an unpleasant history or if there has been any odometer tampering.

CarFax offers both one time use fees and monthly fees. Since you will most likely be checking out several vehicles, choose the CarFax program most suited to your needs. CarFax can be found online at http://www.carfax.com.

VEHICLE INSPECTION

Storage Conditions

You have found your car, talked to the owner, checked CarFax and are on the way to inspect the Ferrari of your dreams. Dealers generally have large garages or showrooms and acceptable addresses, auctions are ill-advised, so the following only applies to cars for sale by owners.

Where and how the current owner stored the car can speak volumes about its life and conditions. Is the car located in a rental space or in a private home? Is the car stored in a garage, carport or just outside with a car cover? Where did this Ferrari spend most of its time?

Here's the ideal where and how scenario:
The Ferrari of your dreams is sitting in a spacious, secure, warm, dry garage with plenty of light, clean cement floors, and no oil, water, or fluid stains under-or around-- the car. There should be no dangerous chemicals stored near the car, and everything in the garage should be neat, clean and organized. There should appear to be plenty of room to open the doors to the vehicle. There should be nothing directly over the car which may at one point of time fall and cause damage. Garage doors should open easily and provide good access to the street. A garage with Ferrari posters, signs, or similar paraphernalia is always a good indication of a careful and proud owner.

There should be no visible spider webs under or around the car. The tires should be properly inflated, and a trickle charger should be in use constantly (the LAST thing one wants to do is to jump start a Ferrari with electronic ignition!!). A car cover is optional in a clean garage but they are still helpful. The car should start almost instantly and not driven until after a few minutes of warm up.

Anything less than the above scenario should serve as an immediate warning. If you feel you should be packing a 45 when walking around the neighborhood, be wary. If you have to help the owner remove boxes from the fenders, move bicycles out of the way and collect dirty laundry from the driver's seat, you know you're in trouble. If the seller is a collector, and you have to help him move six cars to access yours, you can assume your dream car is not a daily driver. If the 308 is sitting in the yard under a plastic tarp, go home. You get the picture.

If the environment is friendly, proceed to look at the car. A long shot, first, from about 20 feet. Do not buy a car after just seeing it at night. Inspect it both in a garage under fluorescent lights and outside in the full sun. The difference of appearance in different light is astounding. Paint flaws, nicks, and scratches appear better under different lights.

An additional hint here: Purchase and take along a copy of Keith Bluemel's "Original Ferrari V8". (To find current purchasing information, simply search the internet). No matter what model of 308, you'll find detailed photos and descriptions of exactly how the original models looked as they came from the factory and the book also includes pictures of the body, interior, trunk, suspension, and engine details. You'll be able to compare your find with photos in the book to see if everything is in place, in good shape, and original.

Another good idea is to take along your own digital camera. This will allow you to return home and further investigate and appraise the car.

EXTERIOR

Body
Overall: Looking at the car from a few feet away can provide some good insights. Does the car sit level? Is the paint even or faded in areas? Are there too many swirls or scratches in the finish? Are the door gaps consistent? Are the panels straight or slightly warped? Does anything seem out of place, out of position, uneven or simply not right? Are the lines, curves, and surfaces crisp? Does it look and feel like it just came off the showroom floor? Good cars simply have a 'feeling' about them which is not easy to define. You'll know it- or feel it- when you see it.

Rust: There are several common rust areas on steel bodied 308s. The common locations are on the rear deck lid and the bottom rear of each door. Check each area carefully. You should also inspect the bottom side of the door on the interior. The later QV cars included additional rust protection, while the early 308 had little to none. Be particularly careful when checking pre-1985 models. Although rust in these areas might not be a deal breaker, it should be taken into account when determining a fair price.

Paint: Factory Ferrari paint during the 308 era was not the greatest, and the newest cars are now over 20 years old. Because of this, repaints are common on 308s. Due to the complex lines, it is very, very difficult to have a 308 body repainted without overspray or other signs of bodywork. Of course it can be done, given enough money. A re-spray, however, is not a bad thing, particularly if well done and in the original color. Ask the owner if you are in doubt. New paint may be due to an accident or other serious damage to the frame or suspension. I would tend not to trust a 308 newly repainted in "resale red" over blue paint.

Emblems: There are emblems in a lot of places on the 308. They can be expensive and annoying to replace. Although not as common as it used to be, people steal emblems, and this can be an issue when looking for a car. Bluemel's book is a great source for determining what and where the emblems should be.

Glass: Windows on the 308 are very expensive. Watch for scratches in the door glass and cracks or pits in the windshield which may prevent the car from passing inspection. If there are cracks, make sure they don't interfere with your vision while driving.

INTERIOR

Odometer Mileage
Mileage figures are often a damned if you do and damned if you don't scenario. While everyone wants to own a "low mileage example", a well maintained, regularly driven, relatively high mileage Ferrari can possibly be a much better buy and end up being much more reliable. A rarely driven, low mileage, mint example may suffer from drying seals, cracked hoses, stiff shocks, moisture in the brakes, oil leaks, and expensive belts that tend to develop a 'set' from being in one position for too long. Even the oil in Koni shocks will solidify if not kept in use.

The key is to try to find a car which is in great original shape but used often enough to keep it reliable. But, mileage figures based on the odometer alone may not be correct. In addition to checking to see if the mileage is accurate, also ask if the odometer has ever been serviced, not just if it's correct. Titles should note if there is any odometer modifications.

The odometers on 308's are very easy to disconnect. This means that you'll have to make an educated guess if one of the previous owners was malicious and greedy enough to do such a thing. One of the main indicators of a false odometer reading can be found using CarFax, which lists mileage at various times. Other clues are typically present as well. Do any of the mileage numbers look out of place with the car's presented history? Another indication might be well worn seats on a very low mileage car. Also, is the engine a mess? Finally, what does the owner's records and documentation tell you? If the condition of the car doesn't match the odometer, make sure to check out the care thoroughly.

Checking the Interior

First, check the seats for originality, wear and tear, and leather quality. Since these cars are at least 20 years old, you should expect to see some wear, especially on the side bolsters of the seats which get rubbed on each entry and exit.

Check the other interior leather parts on the dash and doors. Is it old and cracked? Does it need to be replaced or just reconditioned? Does it have holes in it that can be patched? Also check the knobs and levers. These weren't made of the highest quality material, and often break or come apart after years of service.

Check the carpet. Is it rotted through? Lift the carpet and notice the underside, and check for dampness. Many Ferraris, particularly GTS models, will leak and allow water to collect in the floor pan. How about dust? Does the car appear to have been cleaned regularly, or was it allowed to sit for months on end, collecting dust in hard to reach places?

Instrument Panel Lights and Gauges

The instruments were made by Veglia and are usually fairly accurate. When starting and operating the car, the gauges should all register at least something. If they don't move when the car is started, there is probably something wrong - either with the gauges themselves, or with the sending units. Temperature gauges sometimes have to be given a finger thump to un-peg, and will take several minutes to increase. Also, most of the small gauges are the same as what was standard on the Fiat 850 spiders and coupes of the same era. The wording on the gauges might be slightly different but can't be noticed. Of course most owners know this by now, so the price of a Fiat gauge is often the same as a Ferrari gauge anyway!

Electrical System

The electrical system on the 308 is not the most intelligently designed system. It has its quirks and idiosyncrasies.

Check the fuse panel, which is located on the passenger side, on the bottom part of the dash board (where the glove-box is on most other cars). The fuse panel also contains the relays that may need to be replaced. Relays are standard Bosch units and are also found in VWs, BWMs, Mercedes-Benz, and more. Bad relays can be the cause of a car that won't start, appears to run out of gas (fuel pump relay), or windows and lights that don't operate.

Battery
Is the battery new or fairly old? Luckily, the battery isn't a unique and expensive item, and can be replaced with the appropriate sized battery from just about any auto parts shop. Batteries on Ferraris tend to not last long. This is because the cars aren't driven very often, which causes batteries to be completely drained. When a battery is completely drained, the life expectancy of the battery drops dramatically. The best thing for batteries is a trickle charger, and many dealers install them on new cars, realizing that few Ferraris get driven enough to keep the battery charged properly. Maintaining even voltages is also very important for electronic control units (ECU).

Trunk - Rear Storage
Next, check the "trunk" or "boot". All 308's have a zippered section behind the engine which can store things the approximate size of a large golf bag. This area should be clean, and contain nothing - unless the factory toolkit or luggage is included.

Try opening and closing the zipper a couple of times. It can be snug, but often times, the cover shrinks and the zipper will no longer work. Although this isn't reason for operational concern (it can happen on even the most cared-for vehicle), if you're looking for a show car, this may need fixing or replacing.

If you are wondering where the ECU/ ECM s are, they are below the floor, on the left side of the car underneath a metal plate. And yes, they do fail. And yes, they are very expensive to replace.

Spare Tire
The spare tire, located in the front boot, is a full-size spare. Some Euro versions have a narrow, smaller spare for emergency use only. The jack and associated tools for replacing a flat tire should be stowed underneath the spare tire. Behind the fiberglass covering, which can be removed if necessary, is the brake reservoir. Because the clutch is a manual device, there is no hydraulic assist and no reservoir.

Engine
The engine compartment should be clean. Though a dirty compartment might not signal anything specific, it may show a lack of care by the previous owner. If there are large amounts of oil and grime buildup in areas, it is a sign of possible oil leaks somewhere in the engine. The identification plates and plaques should all be in place.

Clean, yes, but most Ferrari engines leak or have leaked oil. Don't condemn them for this condition unless the oil drip is serious. One place that oil can be a serious problem is around the cam timing belts. Timing belts do not like oil and can deteriorate quickly if soiled. Ask the owner to remove the air filter canister on the right side of the car (usually very easy to do) and this will allow you to inspect oil and dirt deposits in the vicinity of the cam timing belts.

Remove the oil filler cap on the cam cover and check to see that any oil on the inside of the cap is clean. If a head gasket has blown, it will allow water in the oil and cause a very milky appearance to the oil, which in turn can be found on the oil cap. Check the dipstick for proper oil level and clean oil without condensation. Check the water overflow tank for clean antifreeze. Oil can also get into the water as the result of an internal leak, and there may be oil in the water. This will appear as oily "soap suds" in the overflow tank and cap.

Ask the owner when the oil was last changed. Bear in mind that synthetic oils are by far the better oil but still should be changed every 3 to 5 thousand miles. Also, sitting in a garage will allow the oil to accumulate more condensation and break down quicker than if used every day!

CHASSIS

Frame
The frame should be straight and in good condition. If the tire wear is uneven it could be poor suspension alignment or a bent frame. If possible, check for shims in the suspension at the adjustment points to the chassis. If there are noticeably more on one side, a bent frame is likely.

Tires
Check the wear pattern on the tires. Is the inner or outer edge of each tire worn excessively compared to the rest of the tire? This can be a good indication of incorrect alignment, or as mentioned previously, could be indicative of a bent chassis frame. Also check the total tire wear. A good set of four tires isn't cheap, and can be hard to find if the car has the original metric rims.

Suspension
Physically (get down on the floor and underneath the car!!!) examine the suspension by checking for leaks in the shock absorbers or worn bushings (which may be very difficult to spot!). Worn suspension bushings will make the car noisy and "creaky" while driving over bumps. Gently push down on the front and rear bumpers and check the rebound of the car and listen for strange noises. During the test drive try to drive in a variety of settings, from low speed to high speed bumps

(not too large!) and listen for any noises coming from the suspension area.

Accident Damage
Check for accident damage by carefully looking over the bodywork for sand scratches, bondo, overspray, and use a small plastic covered magnet to determine if there is plastic over the steel in suspect areas. But the old trick of using a magnet won't work on the fiberglass cars.

Ask the owner if they know of any previous accident damage. You should already know the answer to this from CarFax report, but just in case CarFax missed something , ask the owner anyway. For example, if an accident wasn't reported to the authorities or the insurance company, it won't show up.

Owner's Manuals
Check that the Owner's Manual and the Warranty Logbook are included with the vehicle. Verify that they are the correct year and they are in good condition. If they are for a different year, inquire why and find out if the originals are available. New manuals and books are available online, but they aren't cheap.

Tool Kit
The tool kit contains many different tools and accessories for the car. Though not essential, they can be expensive to replace if they're not included with the car. The GT4 contained two tool kits.

The first contained the following items:
• Carburettor adjustment wrench
• 8 open ended wrenches (6-22mm)
• Pliers
• 4 Screwdrivers (2 flat, 2 Philips)
• Spark Plug wrench

The second kit contained:
• Tire Jack with ratchet
• Wheel nut wrench
• Spare Alternator belt
• Spare air conditioner belt
• Air pump belt (US versions only)
• Road Hazard Reflective Triangle (Euro versions only)
• Various fuses
• Various bulbs
• Spare spark plugs.

The GTBs and GTSs also contained two toolkits. One is referred to as the "Tool Roll" and the other is the "Tool Bag".

The Tool Roll contained:
- Carb adjustment wrench (carb'd cars only)
- 8 open ended wrenches (6-22mm)
- Pliers
- 4 screwdrivers (2 flat, 2 Philips)
- Spark plug wrench
- Exhaust extensions (for emission analysis) - US Only.

The Tool Bag should contain:
- Tire jack with ratchet
- Wheel nut wrench
- Spare alternator belt
- Spare air conditioner belt
- Air pump belt (US versions only)
- Road Hazard Reflective Triangle (Euro versions only)
- Various fuses
- Various bulbs
- Spare spark plugs.

THE TEST DRIVE

If you have managed to get this far, you are now ready to take the car for a test drive. Don't be surprised if the owner is not happy about this. He'll want to make sure you are an eligible buyer and not a mere tire kicker. It would be wise to carry some sort of proof that you are indeed financially capable of purchasing his pride and joy, before he lets you out on a 'joy' ride. The owner may also want to go with you, and perhaps even drive it first with you as a passenger. All of this is good, because that means the current owner is very concerned about his car and what happens to it. Don't take it personally.

Cold Starting

If possible, ask the dealership or seller to refrain from starting the car for at least several hours before your scheduled inspection and test drive. The reason for this is to make sure there are no cold-starting issues. You can check how the car starts as it would in the morning. Cold starting difficulties are manifold. Problems could involve a low or bad battery, poor starter, loose/frayed/cracked wires, relays, solenoids, spark plugs, distributor, coils and so on. It could also be fuel system problems including bad gas, fuel pump problems, choke mechanisms on carbureted cars or starting solenoids on fuel injected cars. Weak links in the system will show up in cold start conditions much more readily than warm start conditions.

Revolutions Per Minute

When started from cold, what RPM does the tachometer indicate? Did it slow down after it warmed up a little, and you revved the engine a little? Once the engine was warmed up, what did the engine idle at? Make a mental note, but remember that each car is different, and a carbureted version will be different than a GTi which in turn will differ from a QV. All, however, should settle down to a relatively smooth and consistent idle around 700-1000 RPM when warm. Does the alternator light turn off once the engine is revved above 2000 RPM?

Listening to the Engine

Does the engine make any odd noises? If you've never heard a 308 engine, it will sound different than anything you've probably heard before. There will be a slight "whining" noise from the timing belt, as well as a "sucking" sound with the carbureted cars. But there shouldn't be any loud rhythmic tapping noises, screeches, or popping.

Clutch and Transmission

The clutch should feel heavy compared to most modern cars. The gear lever will be hard to move, and when cold, may not want to move into second gear. This is a normal condition. Ferrari transmission boxes must be fully warmed before they operate smoothly. However, when shifting, there should not be any grinding of gears, which may indicate a bad clutch or clutch adjustment problem. Shifting a 308 is a matter of both delicacy and brute force. The gearbox responds to quick, positive, but accurate movements. It will let you know if you mistreat it by making a loud grinding noise.

You should get used to the gating on the shifter. Try not to look down at the gate when shifting. Since first gear is where second gear usually is placed, it is difficult not to glance at the gate to ensure you are in the right gear. The gate is cut with minimal play and no tolerance for sloppy shifting - it pays to be precise.

Brakes

Once underway and at a safe location, test the brakes. Does the car stop in a straight line? Does it shimmy on one side or the other? Does the car jerk unexpectedly? How does the car react to light pedal force? How does it react to heavy/hard braking?

Problems could be warped discs, low brake levels, worn brake pads, worn discs, or faulty calipers. A quick note here—the rear brakes on almost any 308 are equipped with adjusters to retract the pistons. This mechanism often becomes useless and warrants a proper and expensive rebuild from a good brake shop.

Parking brake
The parking brake is a cable operated mechanism that only attaches to the rear wheels. When pulled up, the car should not roll. The parking brakes are part of the rear disc brake mechanism and can be adjusted if necessary.

Acceleration check
Is there any jerking or hesitation during a regular or hard acceleration? For the carbureted cars, this can mean some settings or jets are off. For an early car with mechanical points, they may be jumping and need to be replaced or adjusted. Does the car seem like it has enough power? Full power should come on strongly and smoothly throughout the rev range without any hiccups. To be fair, make sure the car is completely warmed up before making any assumptions. Try accelerating from various speeds and in different gears. Take the car through the entire RPM range (but not into the red zone).

Engine Temp. - Overheating
After warming the car up, and at the end of your test drive, let the car idle while you check over the other areas of the vehicle. Before shutting the car off, come back and check the temperature. Is it still within reason? If not, it could be suffering from overheating due to a wide variety of possible maladies. Does the electric fan kick on when required?

Steering
The steering should be tight. These cars don't have power steering, so there should be almost no play in the steering wheel. They also tend to be "brutes" when driving at slow speed and require more force than a car equipped with power steering. The steering lightens up as the speed increases.

Alignment and Suspension
The car should track straight and not pull from side to side. Note, that there will be some "hunting" when you're driving on a street that has any kind of indentations or ruts. This is caused by the aggressive nature of the tires and the alignment.
While you are driving over bumps or rough pavement, listen for thumps, clunks, and other deep rattles. If they aren't coming from something loose in the interior or engine compartment (which there shouldn't be), it may be an indication of something worn in the suspension - most likely one or more of the various suspension bushings.

Driving Evaluation
Until you get familiar with driving a 308, the off center, long armed and low-down position may seem a bit odd. Take the time to see how you fit - there isn't much manual adjustment in these cars, so if you don't fit, or you don't like the position of

the steering wheel, you may be out of luck. Note that the steering wheel is very close to the instrument pod. If you have large fingers, they may often knock the dash when steering!

Warm Engine Restart

After the test drive, shut down the car, then try starting it again, after about 30 seconds. If there is a problem starting it, it could indicate a "warm start" problem in one of the areas listed above.

THE TEST DRIVE CHECKLIST

At the end of this chapter, I have included a customized test-drive checklist for test driving any of the 308s. Before you go to check out a vehicle, make a copy of this checklist, and take it with you. Fill it out as you go over the vehicle inspection.

Professional Check

Surprisingly, professional checks are rarely done. Even I bought my first 308 without getting a professional mechanic to check the systems. Of course, a professional check isn't required to buy a 308, however, it's just like buying cheap insurance for your purchase. If anything is found, you've just avoided spending a lot of "repair money."

Generally, it will take several hours for a mechanic or other automotive professional to check the car. You should arrange with the current owner or dealership to have the car checked over at a time that is convenient for them.

The professional check will involve putting the car on a lift and checking the underside, checking the cylinder compression, checking the suspension, checking the spark plugs, and on-and-on. It can be a detailed process that can make current owners a bit nervous. Having a stranger climb all over your car is a little disconcerting.

The mechanic MUST be familiar with the Ferrari 308. There are a number of problems specific to the 308 that if you don't know what to look for, the odds of missing the problem are much greater. To avoid missing these potential deal-breakers, make sure the inspector has a good knowledge of the 308 model line. Ask your mechanic to provide a complete check off list of items to be inspected— lists will vary and the more you want him to inspect the more dollars will be spent. Dealers often won't let a third party mechanic examine and probe around their vehicles. If they don't allow an inspection, you should insist on some kind of limited warranty that will allow for a return of the car and a full refund after you have it inspected.

MORE INFORMATION

- Ferrari Market Letter. http://www.ferrarimarketletter.com/ Published by Gerald Roush, it's the best place to start looking for a used Ferrari. The bi-weekly newsletter includes classified ads, articles, coming events and the Asking Price Index. This magazine generally isn't available in book stores or magazine racks. You'll need to subscribe to the print or online version.

- Hemmings Motor News. http://www.hemmings.com/ This is the large yellow magazine that is primarily just a large collection of used car ads for "the collector-car enthusiast." It doesn't specialize in Ferraris, but usually has plenty of ads for them.

- Ferrari Ads. http://www.ferrariads.com/ FerrariAds.com is the classified ad section of FerrariChat.com. The ads include not only cars, but parts, and wanted ads.

- Better Business Bureau. http://www.bbb.org/ Before purchasing a used car from a "non-authorized" dealership, be sure to check for any possible issues with the Better Business Bureau.

- eBay. http://www.ebaymotors.com/ Although it's probably not the best place to search for a used Ferrari, there are many available, and it's a good place to look for current sale prices.

TELEPHONE QUESTIONNAIRE

This is a list of questions you should ask a seller. You can use this form to determine if it's worthwhile to take the vehicle for a test drive and perform additional inspections. Make photocopies of this page, and take notes on the conversation.

Phone Interview	
Seller's name	
Phone number	
Email address	
Where was the ad	
Ad details	
Date/time of call	
Model year	
VIN	
Mileage	
Ext. color	
Int. color	
Odometer OK?	
Asking price	$
How long owned	
Reason for selling	
Past insurance claims	(minor or major accidents, vandalism, robbery, etc.)
Documentation?	(Owner's Manuals, Service History, and Receipts)

Phone Interview (Continued)	
Does it pass emissions	
Transmission OK?	
Exterior condition	any rust, dings, dents, or paint chips?
Paint condition	repaints? when/why? original color?
Interior condition	
Accidents?	Any insurance claims against car?
Title	Clear Title? Salvage Title?
Owner's manuals	
Toolkit	
Mechanical updates or changes	
Wheels and rims	Nicks/dings? Spare tire included?
Last service	(service information)
How many previous owners	
Owner comments	

After the call	
Your general feelings	Your general opinion about the seller and about the car
Test drive scheduled?	date/time:
Directions to the test drive	
Good things about this car	
Bad things about this car	
Notes	

INSPECTION CHECKLIST

Photocopy this checklist and take a blank copy with you when you go to check out a possible car.

General Information and Identification	
Year	
Model	
Mileage	miles/kilometers
VIN	
Serial #	
Engine #	
Market	US / European LHD / RHD
Body	Steel / Fiberglass
Ext. Color	
Int. Color	
Seller	
Asking	$
Phone #	
Location	

Documentation / Maintenance History
Describe any documented maintenance history
.

Circle any Repairs or Replaced Parts within the past 12 months and 5000 miles

Timing Belt	Water Pump	Brakes	Battery
Bearings (belt, etc)	Clutch	Fuses/Relays	Interior
Tires	Paint	A/C	Hoses

Exterior Inspection (page 1)	
Paint	Original / Repainted
Paint Condition	Excellent / Good / Okay / Spider-webs / Cracks / Faded / Panels Match Notes:
Damage	Scratches: Dings/Dents:
Panel Alignment	Hood: Rear Deck Lid: Left Door: Right Door: Roof (GTS): Bumpers:
Bumper Condition	Check for scratches, bends, and dents:
Badges	Hood / Deck lid / Rear / Sides
Glass	Windshield: Rear Window: Door Windows: Side Windows:
Grill Condition	

Exterior Inspection (page 2)	
Rust	Front Wheel Well/Arches: Rear Wheel Well/Arches: Door Panels: Rear Deck Lid: Other:
Roof (GTS)	
Lens Covers	Turn Signals: Fog Lights: Tail/Brake Lights:
Trim	Window Trim: Body Trim:
Louver Fins	Behind Headlights: Hood: Side Windows: Deck Lid:
Rearview Mirrors	
Valence	Front Spoiler: Rear Valence:
Lic. Plate	Euro or US Mounting:
Exhaust Tips	

Frame Inspection	
Alignment	No Accidents Alignment of tires correct Even wearing of properly aligned tires
Rust	Underbody Rust Front Mid Rear Engine Compartment
Cracks	Front Rear Engine Compartment ("buttress connections")

Tires and Wheels	
Wheel/Rim	Scratches/Center/Sizes
	LF:
	RF:
	LR:
	RR:
Tire Wear	Inflation
	Uneven (See Frame Inspection)
	Alignment
	Side Walls
Tire Sizes	Front Tires
	Rear Tires
Spare Tire	Condition
Bolts	Condition
	Locking? Keys Included?

Doors and Door Windows	
Dings	
Trim	No cracks Seals Tightly
Window Operation	Open and Close completely Slow speed usually okay.
Locks	Keys Included: Lock and Unlock from Interior and Exterior: Power Locks:
Trim	Window Trim: Body Trim:
Alignment	Gap/Spacing consistent around edges: Open and Close correctly with little effort: Sagging when opened?
Louvers	Clean Underneath Cracks Locks/Keys

Hood and Deck Lid	
Front Hood	Condition. Check for crease or interior body work Strut Operational Release Mechanism:
Deck Lid	Condition. Struts Operational: Release Mechanism:
Front Louvers	Condition of Front Louvers. Color
Rear Louvers	Engine Louvers Condition Color
Headlight Louvers	Condition of Louvers behind headlights
Open/Close	Release Mechanism Condition Close firmly and completely
Louvers	Clean Underneath Cracks Locks/Keys

Interior		
Dash	Leather Condition (dull, cracks, etc): Seams: Fuse Cover:	
Carpet	Floor mats: Wear (driver and passenger side)	
Seats	Wear/Leather Condition: Reclining/Folding Mechanism: Position (locking in place, etc.):	
Seat Belts	Operation (Extend, Retract, and Lock): Wear:	
Instrument Cluster	Operation: Lighting:	
Buttons/Switches	Mechanism: Faceplates: Operation:	
Door Panels	Leather: Door handles/Locks: Pockets:	
Interior Lights	Operation:	

Lights/Wiper Tests	
Headlights	Open/Close: Lights (R & L): High Beams Parking Lights:
Turn Signals	Left/Right
Emergency Flasher	Flashing:
Seat Belts	Operation(Extend, Retract, and Lock): Wear:
Instrument Cluster	Operation: Lighting:
Brake Lights	
Wiper	Operation (fast/slow): Blade Condition:

Heating & A/C	
Heater	Hot: Fans (check all fan speeds)
A/C	Included: Blows Cold Fans (check all fan speeds)
Vents	Airflow:

Radio/Speakers	
Radio	Make and Model: Includes: AM FM TAPE CD MP3 VIDEO
Operation	Receives: AM FM TAPE CD MP3 VIDEO
Speakers	Door Speakers: Additional Speakers:
Amplifiers	Added components: Mounted correctly:

TEST DRIVE CHECKLIST

After your thorough exterior and interior inspection, take the vehicle for a test drive. Sit in the car and adjust the seats, mirrors, and seat-belt to comfortable positions. Before starting the car, turn off the radio and check all the gauges - make a mental note of the gauge positions.

Start Up	
Cranking	
Gauges	
Exhaust	
Cold Idle	Alternator light
Warm Up	Water Temp: Oil Temp:
Emergency Brake	

Transmission	
Clutch	
Reverse	
1-2 shift	
Neutral	
Gear Changes	

Brakes	
Pedal	Firm or loose? Amount of travel
Pull	Do the brakes pull to one side?
Noise	Grinding or squeaking brakes?
Vibration	Pulsating or vibrating pedal during braking?

Acceleration	
Lower RPM	From complete stop and from rolling stop.
Mid RPM	Accelerating from medium speed (like might be used when passing)
High RPM	Acceleration is steady and strong even as you approach the "yellow line"?

Handling and Noise	
Handling	Does the car handle well? Is the steering and suspension "tight" and not loose or bouncy?
Noises	Is there any unusual suspension noise? Is there any unusual engine noise?
Roof Fit	On GTS models, check that the roof fits correctly, and the clamps securely hold the removable top.

PROFESSIONAL INSPECTION CHECKLIST

Lift Inspection

Have a certified (and preferably insured) mechanic perform a complete inspection of the underside of the vehicle. The use of a lift is normally required. Look for signs of fluid leaks, including oil and coolant. Underside inspection should look for physical damage resulting from any prior accidents or collisions. Look for parts that appear new when compared to the other areas.

Mechanic Inspection

General Engine Condition	
Original Engine?	Matching numbers:
New Parts:	Recent Replacements or repairs?
Cleanliness	
Notes & Comments	

Oil Leaks	
Bottom/Top	Around Oil Pan and lower gaskets, valve covers, etc.
Distributor	
Front Seals	
Hoses	Condition of hoses and clamps
Misc. or "slung" oil	Oil level and check for slung or recent oil

Coolant	
Radiator Leaks	Cracks on upper/lower sections
Water Pump	
Hoses	Upper and lower hoses - condition of rubber and clamps
Misc.	Fluid level okay, system holds pressure, clean fluid, fan works

Electrical	
Battery Condition	
Wires, Cables & Clamps	check for cracks, corrosion, loose wires, etc.
Fuse Box & Fuses	
Alternator	
Distributor	Points
Ignition & Starter System	
Lighting System	Interior and exterior lights and lamps

Air Conditioner	
Compressor	Cracks on upper/lower sections
Freon	
Belts	Upper and lower hoses - condition of rubber and clamps

Brakes	
Break Wear	Pads and discs
Brake Fluid	
Master Cylinder	Upper and lower hoses - condition of rubber and clamps
Brake Lines	

Engine Inspection	
Spark Plugs	Are they carbon or oil fouled?
Cylinder Compression	1: 5: 2: 6: 3: 7: 4: 8:
Oil	Consistency and color of oil?
Coolant	Condition of the coolant. Presence of oil.

Exhaust System	
Muffler Condition	Check for rust and aftermarket muffler.
Catalytic Converter	
Oxygen Sensors	

Steering and Suspension	
Shocks and Springs	
Steering Rack	
Wheel Bearings	
Bushings	
CV Joints and Boots	

Frame Inspection	
Muffler Condition	Check for rust and aftermarket muffler.
Catalytic Converter	
Oxygen Sensors	

CHAPTER 5 *The Purchase*

Determining the Value / Pricing

Purchase Price and Value

The Ferrari 308s are traditionally one of the most inexpensive Ferraris you can purchase. At the time of this writing, you could purchase a GT4 in acceptable condition for as little as $15,000. You could also find a top condition 308QV or Fiberglass 308 GTB for $40,000. Depending on what you're looking for, and what you can spend, there should be something available in a wide range of prices.

In addition to the purchase price, you should also consider the cost of repairs and maintenance and weigh them accordingly. Because maintenance on a poor condition Ferrari can be almost as much as the total price of the car, you really have to investigate to make sure that you spend the correct amount of money up front.

You should also weigh your needs versus your wants. You may want a QV, but your budget will barely get you into a marginal example. It will often make sense to get a better fuel-injected car, at the same price. Sure the power won't be there, but you'll be happier with the car and it will be in better condition and easier to maintain. Or, because the GTS versions generally cost more, is the removable roof really one of your requirements? Try to get what you want, but don't short change a good car.

Figure out a high estimate by looking at the asking prices in the magazines such as Ferrari Market Letter, Kelly's Blue Book, Hemmings Motor, and Sports Car Market. Another great price guide can be found in Cavallino magazine. You'll find that most dealers, insurance agents and lenders use the values as published in Cavallino as their guidelines. Cavallino updates the prices six times a year with every new edition of the magazine. Cavallino is available via subscription only. The Ferrari Market Letter has an excellent feature called the "Asking Price Index". The API lists the average asking price for the cars in the Ferrari Market Letter.

This is an excellent indicator of the trends in pricing, but should not be used to directly relate how much you should pay for a Ferrari, other than that you should try to pay less than the current average asking price.

Ever since the Ferrari "boom" in the late 80's and early 90's, Ferrari owners have often wanted more for their cars than they paid. This was due to people looking at Ferrari ownership as an investment. The only investment that should be considered when purchasing a 308 is how much fun one is going to get for the money. Get the idea of profit out of your purchasing process.

If you're bidding on a car in an auction, determine the maximum you'd pay for the car, and stick with your pre-determined amount. It's very easy to get carried away in the "heat of bidding" and bid more than a vehicle is worth, but if you have a predetermined price, it's easier to stop and know that the high bidder paid more than the car was worth. Remember, auctions are not the recommended way to buy your first Ferrari any way!

Resale value

If you're looking to purchase a 308 as an investment, there are many more profitable and less-risky investments. Though used Ferraris tend not to depreciate as quickly as other makes of cars, they will probably not increase in value. The days of the late 80's are gone for good, and the prices have stabilized to a normal value.

Also consider any upgrades or modifications you put on the car. You will probably not get your money back, and in fact, the resale value may be hurt by your changes. For example, take a 308 that's been "race-prepped". All the changes and enhancements made may amount to tens of thousands of dollars. Yet, because the demand for such a car is relatively low, you'll probably have to take five to ten thousand off the sale price! What will help your resale value are the same things that your are looking for during your search. Good documentation, quality maintenance, and a caring owner. These things keep the resale value up.

Gray Market Cars - Euro Cars

A "gray market" car is a European version of the car that was imported into the United States by someone other than Ferrari SpA or Ferrari North America. This means some other distributor or private party is responsible for the importation of the vehicle. It is usually done with a fair amount of paperwork between the importer of the car and the U.S. Department of Transportation. It is also important to note that gray market cars are not illegal - only that they were imported through "non-traditional" methods.

For all practical purposes, any Euro car that you find in the U.S. can be considered a "gray market" car. Euro cars in the U.S. were imported by either private owners or small distributors that bought the vehicles in Europe, then imported them. The regulations and requirements for importing a car can be confusing and difficult to manage. More information on importing requirements can be found at: http://www.nhtsa.dot.gov/cars/rules/import/.

In some situations, you have to be very careful when purchasing a gray market car. There are often issues with local Motor Vehicle Departments when trying to register these cars. The VINs on imported cars (and even the early US 308's) confuse most DMV computers and personnel. Insurance companies have also been known to have difficulties with gray market cars.

Purchasing a Euro car imported into the U.S. does have some risks that you should be aware of. Most importantly, make sure you have enough documentation to support that the car is legal and DOT approved. These are sometimes referred to as "federalization papers" or "DOT and EPA papers" and should contain information on where the safety and emissions changes necessary for importation were completed. If the current title of the car is in the same state that you're registering it, you probably won't have an issue with titling and registering the car. But, if it's in a different state, check with your local DMV before buying the car.

If you have difficulty finding the details on a gray market car, you will need to contact the Department of Transportation directly. They may have the information you're looking for on file. If not, check with your local DMV to see if you'll have any problem registering your vehicle.

Negotiating The Deal
Before you start narrowing your search, be prepared for the negotiations that will take place. It doesn't matter if you're talking with a dealer or private party, you still need to be prepared to negotiate your deal. Preparation is the key to successful negotiating. And successful negotiating can save you thousands of dollars.

To start with a positive negotiating position, have your source of funding completed and ready to go. With the ability to say "I have the cash at the bank," or "My loan is pre-approved," you can show that you're serious about purchasing the car, and that the seller should spend the time necessary to complete the deal.

The best negotiating tool is knowledge. If you're familiar with current market prices and actual sale values, maintenance procedure prices (especially for needed maintenance), what factors are motivating the sale, and the condition of the vehicle, you are in an excellent position for determining the true value of the car. Next, you'll need to figure out three numbers. First, determine the absolute lowest price that you honestly think the seller would accept. This number is where you'll start your "first offer." It's ok if it seems low, that's why it's your first offer. Second, determine a price that you think would be the most fair for both you and the seller, with a slight leaning in your favor. This price is what you should try to make - your goal price. The third number is the most you will pay for the car. If negotiations go even one penny above this price, you have to walk away. *The ability to walk away at a certain price point is your most powerful tool.*

You should use the condition of the car to your advantage. There is always something wrong or not perfect about *any* car, and by letting the owner know about the possible problems with professional demeanor (and you can be sure he already knows about the problems too) you can show that you don't have "Red Fever." Be careful not to insult the owner, but let it be known that you saw the issue and it matters to you.

One of the largest bargaining chips is the status of Major Maintenance schedules. If the car needs a 30k mile check-up, or hasn't had any major service in the past couple years, the value of the car decreases because it can be a $3,000-$5,000 investment to get the service completed.

Be patient and don't appear too anxious. There should be no time-limit. If the seller is pushing too hard to get the sale, step away and determine what's the cause of the rush. Don't be bullied into buying a car you're not sure about. If you're not comfortable with the deal in any way, start looking for another car. The financial implications of purchasing a "lemon" are too great to risk.

Remember that used car dealers are some of the best negotiators. They do this for a living, so be prepared and stand your ground. You both have something to get from the deal - they sell a car, and you get a 308. Private parties can be easier to deal with, but your goals should be the same.

BUYING METHODS

Cash
Hey, if you can pay cash, go for it, but don't forget to think about the opportunity cost of the cash. At the low interest rates available now, this can be worthwhile. But you'll have to weigh the loan rate and total cost versus what you could make with the same money.

Financing
If you're like most people, you don't have $25,000 lying around to purchase a used car. Other than asking a rich relative, you're going to need financing. Depending on your credit report, this can be anywhere from a short, simple process, to a week

long ordeal in the depths of financing hell. Get a copy of your credit report before applying for your loan. Check it for any incorrect entries or problems. If there are any, get them corrected before beginning the application process. Your credit report is about the only basis that a lending institution has when evaluating you for a loan.

The amount of monthly payment you can afford will help determine how much you can spend on the car. The important factors are the amount of the loan, the payback period (usually 4, 5 or 7 years) and the interest rate of the loan.

To calculate the monthly payment you can use one of the many online payment calculators or one of the free downloadable programs. To make things quicker, I've included a simple chart of monthly payments for a variety of loan amounts, interest rates and loan terms. These are just estimates.

Now you'll need to find a lending institution that fits your needs. Banks, credit unions, vehicle lenders and mortgage lenders are the typical providers for used car loans. Make sure you shop around to get the best rate.

	6%	7%	8%	9%	10%	11%
20k 5yr	$386	$396	$405	$415	$425	$435
20k 7yr	$292	$302	$311	$322	$332	$342
25k 5yr	$483	$495	$507	$519	$531	$543
25k 7yr	$365	$377	$390	$402	$415	$428
30k 5yr	$580	$594	$608	$630	$637	$652
30k 7yr	$438	$453	$468	$483	$498	$514
35k 5yr	$676	$693	$710	$727	$744	$761
35k 7yr	$511	$528	$543	$563	$581	$599

Banks

For a variety of reasons, most traditional banks don't offer automotive loans for vehicles older than a few years. Because even the newest 308 is twenty years old, your chances of financing a 308 through your local bank branch is slim-to-none. And, if they do make the loan to you, it would be at a higher rate than is available through other providers. That doesn't mean you shouldn't investigate their rates and loan packages. If your bank is flexible, and you're on friendly terms with the loan officer, it's not impossible.

Credit Unions

Credit unions are usually more flexible when it comes to used car loans and often have rates much lower than traditional banks. Most require you to be a member of the credit union to request a loan, but for many institutions, the requirements to join are minimal. Check in your phone book or online for possible credit union deals in your area.

Vehicle Loan Providers

Vehicle loan providers are lending institutions that specialize in loans for new and used cars. Their rates tend to be competitive, and they usually have a large variety of options and loan types. Check online for reputable lenders.

Mortgage Financing

Another good way of financing is to use a second mortgage, also known as a home equity loan. In addition to the lower interest rates, you might be able to take the interest as a tax deduction.

Be sure to check with your accountant or tax attorney for that kind of information. Also, remember you are paying interest on a long term note, meaning the total financing cost will be much higher.

Leasing

Leasing is available for used cars, including older 308's, but in nearly all cases, it doesn't make financial sense. If you plan on keeping the 308 you've searched for longer than a year, you should probably go with traditional financing.

The Dealership

Most dealerships offer some type of financing. If you're purchasing the car from a dealer with a good reputation, see if they offer a competitive rate with low fees. If they can beat your other possibilities, it could make the loan process easier and quicker.

Insurance

Contrary to what most people think, insuring your Ferrari 308 isn't outrageously expensive or extraordinarily difficult to find. You can save yourself a lot of money and avoid potential problems by shopping around to find insurance that fits your needs. That said, it makes sense to use the same insurer as your other vehicles and home insurance.

Insurance requirements vary greatly between companies. When asking for a quote, be sure to ask about limitations and requirements for coverage. For example, some require that the car always be stored in a locked garage, or limit the amount of mileage you can put on your 308.

Traditional Insurance

Most large insurance companies will charge you a larger premium when compared to the specialty insurance providers. Some won't even consider insuring a Ferrari of any kind. However, this isn't always the case. Check with your current insurance agent to get a quote on insuring your 308 at a variety of deductibles.

Specialty Insurance

Depending on how, where, and when you drive your 308, you may qualify for one of the specialty insurance companies. These policies are generally for limited use vehicles (not "daily drivers") with mileage restrictions. Because these policies are designed specifically for exotic or custom vehicles, the rates are below rates of traditional insurers. These policies tend to have more restrictions, so make sure you read the fine-print and that you can use your 308 as you intend.

Some insurers offer "agreed value" policies, where they insure your car for an agreed upon value that is not based on generic lists of "market values". If your 308 is worth more than what the insurance company says, it is very important to have an agreed value before any claims.

Track/Racing Insurance

The 308 makes a great track car and it's very tempting to race. If you are going to use your 308 either on the track or in any type of race, it is a very good idea to make sure that your insurance will cover you in case there are any incidents. Tracking your 308 can be very risky, and doing it without insurance is completely irresponsible. If your standard policy does not cover racing, you'll need to supplement it with track specific coverage.

Insurers

The following is a list of some (not all) insurers of Ferrari automobiles. Contact their national office or go to their websites for information on local agents that can help you obtain a quote for the coverage you need.

AAA	http://www.aaa.com	
Acordia	http://www.acordia.com	800-648-1600
American Hobbyist	http://www.americanhobbyist.com	800-395-4835
ANPAC	http://www.anpac.com	800-333-2860
Grundy	http://www.grundy.com	800-338-4005
Hagerty	http://www.hagerty.com	800-922-4050
Leland West	http://www.lelandwest.com	800-237-4722
Parish Heacock	http://www.parishheacock.com	800-274-1804
Progressive	http://www.progressive.com	800-776-4737
State Farm	http://www.statefarm.com	

CHAPTER 6   *Owner's Guide*

You did it! You bought your "new" Ferrari 308! You brought it home, and it's sitting patiently in your garage. What do you do now!? What should you do, and more importantly, what should you definitely not do? This chapter will help familiarize you with all the important points of Ferrari ownership.

THINGS YOU NEED

Yes, your new 308 may have set you back in the financial area, but there are a few things you'll need to buy right away. These items will help you in most areas of ownership and maintenance, allowing you to keep your car in pristine operating condition. Some of the items may have been included with the car when you purchased it, but if you're missing some, you'll need to purchase them as soon as possible. Many of the items are available from numerous sources, both new and used. Like shopping for the 308, it's best to shop around to find the best prices and the best product.

Owner's Handbook

The first thing you should do is *read* the Owner's Handbook (also known as the Owner's Manual) that came with your car. If your 308 didn't come with the owner's manual (and many don't) go buy one. Go buy one now. It will save you a lot of time and frustration trying to figure out how to do numerous things with your new car. The owner's manual describes the basic operation and proper care of your vehicle. It includes the general specifications, running and operating instructions, maintenance procedures, and electrical diagrams. Nearly every basic operating procedure is described, ranging from starting the car and parking it to towing the car and washing it. Without the manual you may find a lot of little annoyances with some of the miscellaneous features and operations.

Each model has a slightly different owner's manual, but the content is very similar. If you have a manual, but it is off a year or two, but within the same model range (carbureted, injected, or QV) then you are probably okay. If you want to enter your car in a Concours d'Elegance or a similar competition, you'll have to find the correct manual for your car.

In addition to the officially published version of the manual produced by Ferrari, there are scanned copies available from a number of sources on the Internet. Although the scanned copies are of medium to poor quality, they do have the content you'll need to help understand your car. For high quality official copies of the manual you can check places such as FerrariBooks.com, FerrariLiterature.com and FerrariStuff.com. Ebay.com often has people selling both digital and bound copies.

A word here about Ferrari copyrights: Ferrari is very aggressive about protecting copyrights on names, material, designs, logos, and more. Purchasing an unlicensed copy of an owner's manual, parts or shop manual, or any other material originally copyrighted by Ferrari may be illegal.

Workshop Repair Manual

The workshop repair manual is specifically for the serious do-it-yourselfer. The workshop manual lists nearly all of the technical specifications, tolerances, and torque settings for the engine, cooling system, transmission and chassis. Though this manual isn't required, it can help with any specific questions you may have about internal components.

Like the owner's manual, there are both official and scanned (photocopied) versions available. The official copies are relatively rare and are no longer produced by Ferrari, so finding a used copy can be both difficult and expensive. In most cases a scanned copy is sufficient.

Parts Manual

The parts manual is the companion book to the workshop repair manual. It contains the list of nearly every component and its corresponding part number. Knowing the part number of the part you're looking for can be extremely helpful when trying to order a replacement. If you do any serious work, a parts manual will be very beneficial. The parts manual also contains "exploded views" of many of the major and minor systems in the 308. Although there isn't step-by-step instruction for assembly or disassembly of the systems, the exploded view can be invaluable for understanding how the system goes together.

Tools

Even if you don't plan on doing any serious work on your 308, you should be prepared for any minor care that may need to be done. You should have enough tools to perform the basic maintenance tasks as well as most emergency procedures.

Low Profile Floor Jack

Typically the clearance for a 308 is under five inches, which makes fitting a standard floor jack under the correct jacking point difficult. Since most floor jacks and nearly all "bottle" jacks won't even come close to fitting under the car, you have two choices - a new low profile jack or a few 2x6's.

A low profile hydraulic jack makes the limited clearance a non-issue. There are numerous low profile jacks on the market with prices starting under $100, all the way up to almost $1,000 for light-weight aluminum models. Although they're pricey, they make lifting your car for basic tire changes or getting better access to the underside of the engine more convenient.

If you already have a standard hydraulic jack that doesn't fit under the car and you don't want to buy another jack, there is another solution. By placing two or four 2x6 boards on the ground and driving your 308 onto them, you can get an additional 2 inches clearance. Just make sure you align the boards correctly under the tires when driving up on them, and make sure they are placed correctly when lowering the car back down.

Toolkit

For some reason, a large percentage of 308's don't have their original toolkits. The factory toolkit contains a number of useful tools that can help when you're doing standard maintenance and if you're ever stuck on the side of the road.

If you don't have a factory toolkit, or can't find one at a reasonable price, you can make your own. In addition to the standard assortment of screwdrivers you should also include at the following:

- socket wrench and sockets that fit at least the tire nuts and spark plugs
- a variety of fuses and relays
- a small and light-weight scissors-type jack
- motor oil - at least a couple quarts for emergencies
- spare bulbs for exterior lights
- miscellaneous tools such as pliers, wire cutters, etc.
- belts for the alternator and air conditioner
- flares and road hazard triangles if you're feeling unlucky

Fire Extinguisher

Because the 308 operates with two separate ignition systems (one ECU for each bank of 4 cylinders), if one fails the car will still run but with reduced power. Since 4 cylinders will be dumping unburned fuel through your exhaust, a fire can start quickly. The "Slow Down" lights help prevent this, but if you don't stop immediately, or the lights don't illuminate, you're going to have a fire.

Having a $200 halon fire extinguisher can save your car from burning to the ground. You should have a fire extinguisher mounted inside your car and another in your garage. Only use halon type extinguishers. Chemical-based extinguishers are extremely corrosive and will damage nearly every engine component if it's sprayed. The halon extinguishers work by removing the oxygen around a fire, thus preventing the fire from "breathing." They are more expensive than chemical alternatives, but well worth the extra price.

Halon extinguishers are available in most motorsports catalogs and online. You should get at least a 2.5 pound canister, and if you have the room, a 3 or 5 pound is even better. The 2.5 pound version can be mounted in a number of inconspicuous places including behind the driver's seat on GTB's or just in front of the passenger seat (right below where the passenger's knees would be). Mounting kits and instructions on how to make your own are available from several places on the Internet.

Washing and Detailing Equipment

To keep your car's finish looking good, you'll need to dedicate time to caring for and cleaning the entire exterior. While there isn't anything special about washing and detailing a 308, any minor mistakes or problems can become very expensive. To keep accidents to a minimum, it's a good idea to have a dedicated set of detailing accessories. A clean bucket from anywhere will work fine, but dedicated sponges and chamois will reduce the chances of foreign particles and contaminants damaging your 308's paint. Several specialty automotive catalogs sell "starter packs" that contain just about everything you'll need to start taking excellent care of the exterior and interior of you car. And, at around $50, they're not that expensive.

FINDING A QUALITY FERRARI MECHANIC

Unless you're a mechanic, or a very gifted shade-tree mechanic with lots of time, you're going to need a quality mechanic to work on your car. The process of finding a trustworthy and knowledgeable mechanic for your Ferrari is a little more important than with your other cars. The consequences of having an incompetent or ignorant mechanic work on your 308 can cost a lot of money.

There are basically four types of shops: dealerships, independents, chain stores, and specialty shops. Dealerships have authorized repair facilities, but can be expensive and slower. Independent shops are more common but knowledge and trustworthiness can vary. National chain stores that provide generic service for nearly all types of cars but are usually not the correct choice for Ferrari work. Specialty shops typically focus on a single system or component of a car. For example a radiator or water-pump rebuild shop, or a shop that focuses only on suspension alignment.

In most cases, if you purchased your 308 from an authorized Ferrari dealership, the dealership is your best bet. Ferrari North America regularly inspects and monitors its authorized dealers to make sure they maintain high customer satisfaction and quality. The prices will tend to be higher because of the training and "authorized" status.

Independent shops are great if you are familiar with them and they are familiar with the intricacies of the 308. The best way to find a dependable independent shop is to ask someone else for a referral. Check online on the FerrariList or FerrariChat forums. Search the archives or start a new thread and ask about a particular shop. If you have a local Ferrari club, ask their members. They usually have many opinions on the topic of mechanics.

If you are a do-it-yourselfer, or you want some specific repairs or modifications to your car, a specialty shop is a good choice. Though they might not be experts on the 308, or even Ferraris in general, they are nearly always experts in their specific fields. If you're looking for high performance parts or hard-to-find replacements, a specialty shop will be your best bet. And in some cases, your independent (or even authorized dealership) may work with a specialty shop on your behalf.

After you've narrowed your choice down to a few specific shops, do a little research. See if there are any outstanding complaints about the shop at the Better Business Bureau or your State Attorney General. Next, visit the shops in person and talk to the owner and/or the head mechanic. As with purchasing your Ferrari, the type of environment is also important to a garage. Is it clean, well lit, with proper lifts? Do the mechanics seem to be professionals or kids off the street? Ask about their knowledge and experience with Ferraris and 308's in particular. Find out how often they work on exotics. Ask to take a tour of their shop. Trust your personal impressions and feelings. If you don't feel right, you don't need any other reason not to patronize a particular shop.

DAY-TO-DAY CARE

The day-to-day use of your 308 isn't that much different than any other car. There are a few special items that we'll discuss here, but for the most part, common sense should win.

Fueling
All 308's use unleaded fuel. In nearly all cases you should put the "premium" gasoline in your car.

Octane
Octane is added to gasoline to decrease its susceptibility to pre-detonation. Pre-detonation occurs in engines when the heat and pressure generated by the compression cycle (when the piston compresses the air-fuel mixture in the combustion chamber) cause the air-fuel mixture to ignite BEFORE the spark from the spark plug would normally ignite the mixture. The "pinging" noise that is heard in some engines is a sign of pre-detonation.

The compression ratio on the 308s ranges from 8.8:1 to 9.2:1. While these values are above the average vehicle, they are nowhere near the values used in race cars. (often above 11:1 ratios!). Remember, that more octane does NOT add power to your car, it only decreases the possibility of a pre-detonation.

The factory recommends 87 octane for most of the cars, but because of ethanol and other ingredients, and the possible damage that can be caused by a pre-detonation, most owners tend to put at least a 91 octane fuel in their car.

Fuel Additives
There are a variety of fuel additives on the market that treat several different problems. Cleaners, boosters, and emissions reducers are all readily found at your local auto shop or gas station. These products promise a lot, but a few are actually helpful, and some are even detrimental.

Most cleaning additives are useful for both carbureted and fuel injected cars. The theory is that the additives clean the small nozzles that control fuel flow into the engine (either the jets in a carburetor, or the injectors in an injected car). There are a variety of offerings from GumOut, RedLine, and Chevron. Do they work? In some cases, yes. But don't count on it!

Octane Boost should only be used when you can't find at least 87 octane fuel, or when your engine is experiencing pre-detonation due to "bad" gas. Pinging is very hard on the engine, so boosting the octane rating with these types of additives will help. Remember that higher octane does not give your engine more power.

Emission reducing additives are common, but their effectiveness is debatable. If you're having difficulty passing emissions testing requirements, then you probably have a larger issue with your 308. Masking the problem temporarily may cause the underlying issue to deteriorate, usually leading to even larger repair bills. You'd be better off taking the car to a good mechanic and investigate the cause of the excessive emissions.

Another good product is gas stabilizer. While we'd all like to drive our cars everyday, it probably won't happen, particularly after the new wears off. Adding a gas stabilizer to the fuel means that if left undriven or unstarted in the winter months, the gas will not go to varnish as quickly and the car will start. Bad gas is difficult stuff to clean out of fuel injectors and fuel lines!

Checking The Oil
The oil should be checked each time you fill up the gas tank. It takes only a small amount of effort, and can reduce any nasty "low oil" surprises. You should check your oil when your engine is warmed up, and you've left it off for approximately five minutes. For the exact procedure on checking the oil level consult your Owner's Handbook.

Engine oil is sometimes burnt off in small amounts during heavy or extended driving. This is usually not a problem unless the loss is extreme. Ferraris have always tended to burn more oil than normal cars, but if more than one quart per 1000 miles under normal driving conditions (not high speed events or mountain driving, which will increase oil burning) have it checked out.

We have found that the best oil to use is Mobil 1 20W50. This is a personal decision, but oil is the lifeblood of the Ferrari engine, so don't skimp.

Oil additives, such as friction reducers, should never be used. These additives are basically like "Teflon" for your engine. The down side is that they also coat non-moving parts of the engine and oil passages. This can cause unwanted restriction of oil flow in critical sections of the engine. Reducing oil flow, and the resulting reduction in oil pressure will cause far more damage than the slightly lowered friction on moving parts.

Checking the Coolant
You should check the coolant every few hundred miles. The coolant overflow tank is on the driver's side rear of the engine compartment. The coolant level should never be lower than two inches below the filler hole at the top of the container.

Check with your Owner's Handbook for precise instructions. It is important to note that you should only check the coolant level when the engine is cool. Opening the cap while the engine is warm can be very dangerous.

DETAILING AND WASHING

Detailing and washing are very important to the appearance of your 308. You should take care to correctly wash your car because any damage will be costly. By following the information detailed below, as well as the manufacturer's suggested uses for the products, you can keep your 308 looking new and shiny. If the following sections don't give you enough information, there are several books available that examine washing and detailing in great depth. The "Additional Information" section lists the books and website that can help in your search of concours level detailing.

Exterior - Wash
We'll start with the first rule of washing any exotic car: Always wash your Ferrari by hand! NEVER let a machine touch the paint on your car! To understand the correct method of washing your Ferrari, examine what you are trying to accomplish. The goal is to remove the dirt, dust, oil, grime, and other foreign material off the exterior surface, without damaging the paint. Microscopic scratches (and some bigger ones too) are introduced into the paint surface whenever foreign material is moved along the surface. Think sandpaper. These ultra-fine scratches cause the paint and clear-coat to become dull and lose their shine.

The perfect method of washing would be to pick each microscopic piece of foreign material directly off the paint, without moving it around on the paint and putting microscopic scratches on the surface of the paint. Since this is impossible, we must try the next best thing, which is using water and soap to lift the material off the surface of the paint, and move it to the ground with as little scratching as possible. Before beginning, make sure you have everything necessary to rinse, wash, rinse, and dry your car. This will include soap, sponge or other type of non-abrasive cleaning utensil, and a towel or chamois for drying. All of the items should be completely clean.

There are dozens of types and brands of car wash soaps on the market, and which one you choose will be up to you. Just make sure that you use a high-quality product that is non-abrasive. You should definitely stay away from soaps that were not specifically made for washing cars. A good soap works by attaching itself too, and surrounding, the dirt particles, lifting it away from the painted surface. Never use dishwashing or laundry soaps - these can ruin the finish by dissolving the wax and clear-coat! They're not designed for lifting dirt off painted and waxed surfaces; they're for cleaning food off plates.

Some of the soaps that have been recommended by knowledgeable Ferraristi include: Griots Garage Car Wash, TurtleWax ZipWax Car Wash, and Zymol Natural Concentrated Auto Wash. If you're familiar with a product and you're happy with it, stick with it.

A large bucket and a good large and clean sponge are next. Fill the bucket with soap and water and put the sponge in it to soak up the soapy water. Instead of a sponge you can also use a "wash mitt" which is basically a glove with a sponge attached to it.

Rinse the car with a lot of water. Try to get as much dirt off the car as possible using the water only. A special spray nozzle is acceptable, as is using your thumb to make a concentrated spray in a particular area. But don't put too much focus on the spray - you want to loosen the dirt, not grind it into the paint. One thing to look out for is the "open" areas around GTS versions. If there are areas that tend to leak, don't spray directly into them at odd angles. They *will* leak. If you know you have areas that leak, put towels in the car before you start to avoid getting the leather and carpet wet.

After you've removed as much dirt as possible with water alone, use the sponge to clean the stubborn dirt. Use very gentle motions and a lot of soapy water. Remember, you want to use just enough force to remove the dirt, but not scratch the finish. Start at the top and work your way down. Keep the water flowing while you scrub to allow the dirty soap and water to be carried away. While you're washing, you also want to avoid letting a different section of the car dry as it will leave water spots.

Once the entire painted surface is clean, rinse the entire car to make sure you removed all the excess soap. You can then start to dry it off using either a 100% cotton terry cloth, a natural chamois, or a synthetic chamois. Which one to use is a personal preference, but whatever one you use, make sure it is clean.

If you run across any dirty areas that you missed with the sponge, spot clean the area with the soapy water and sponge, then rinse and dry.

Wash your wheels and tires last, as they will be the dirtiest part of your car. There are several wheel and tire cleaners on the market that will work on your 308's wheels. Make sure they are non-abrasive and work on the wheels that you have. Some people like to make their tires glossy or "wet" by putting "interior protectors" on them. This is not recommended because any products with petroleum distillates in them (including motor oil) will decay the tire's rubber, causing them to discolor, dry-out and crack. If you want clean tires, use products specifically designed for tires; silicone or water based products tend to be the best.

Exterior - Wax/Polish

Waxing and polishing your 308 serves two purposes. First, it makes the paint appear glossy, deep, and slightly wet. Secondly, it protects the paint from scratches and exposure to the environment (water, dirt, oil, light, etc). Traditionally, this has been accomplished with some type of natural wax, but recently synthetic products have begun to replace wax.

If you're using a traditional wax you should only use a high-quality carnauba based wax. Local auto stores may have wax of high enough quality, but if you're unsure, check some of the specialty car care catalogs. Synthetic waxes are available and have nearly all of the qualities of carnauba based waxes. The difference is that the synthetics tend to last longer than carnauba because they are able to bond directly with the paint. The appearance of synthetics is almost as good, if not better in some cases, than the carnauba.

Follow the instructions on the package for applying and removing wax. Do not use heavy force when applying wax. Some people prefer using an orbital buffer to apply and remove wax. This can be dangerous if you missed any dirt, or are unfamiliar with the proper use of a buffer. Set aside time to do it correctly by hand and you'll be happier with the results.

Interior

To keep your interior looking its best, try to keep it in good condition by regularly vacuuming and dusting. This will not only keep your 308 looking good, it will reduce the amount of time you'll have to spend when you want to do a full detailing.

Start by taking out any removable interior items such as floor mats. Clean them outside of the car, and finish cleaning the rest of the interior before putting them back. Next, clean any areas that are actually dirty. Places such as the door jambs, door sills, foot wells and under the seats. You can use a damp cloth to remove the excess dirt that builds up in these areas. Vacuum every surface, crevice, and nook and cranny that you can see. You want to get rid of every piece of dirt possible.

Make sure you get the seats, corners of the seats, behind the seats, and underneath the seats. Move the seats all the way forward and backward during cleaning to reach all areas. Use the extension and other attachments that came with the vacuum to help reach the trouble areas. Vacuum the dashboard to get any dust, but be careful not to scratch the leather with the vacuum hose attachments.

If your vacuuming doesn't get the carpets clean, you'll need to use a carpet or upholstery cleaning solution. Depending on the size of the dirty area, you can use either a spot type cleaner (usually a spray on/rub-off solution) or a full-blown carpet shampoo. Just be sure to check the products for any possible discoloration by testing it in a small and inconspicuous spot before using all over. Again, following the instructions on the package will yield the best results.

After cleaning the carpet, you'll need to turn your attention to the leather. The seats and dash are leather. The dash shouldn't be very dirty, but your seats are probably worn a bit. For the dash, I recommend using a good quality leather "wipe" that will clean the leather gently. Your seats may require more attention, depending on the condition and amount of use you put them through. Start by cleaning the leather with leather cleaner. Again, use a small area on the back of the seat to test for possible discoloration. Follow the directions on the leather cleaner.

After the leather is cleaned and dried, follow up with a leather conditioner. Conditioning the leather will help it last longer, as well as making it look better. Leather is a strong material and there's no reason that it shouldn't be in great condition after 30 years. Take care of it, and it will last.

Often the driver's side bolsters show a lot of wear. If they're cracking or showing signs of severe wear, you're probably in need of a re-dye. Re-dying the leather will require a stripping of the original dye, and applying new dye. This process can take many hours, and although many owners do it themselves, professionals often get better results. Before attempting this yourself, check online for descriptions of the process.

Engine
One of the more exciting parts of a 308 is its engine, and showing off the engine is part of owning an exotic car. But, if the engine isn't as clean as the exterior, it isn't nearly as impressive. Keeping your engine clean is important.

Before cleaning your engine bay make sure all electrical connections are covered correctly. Getting water or cleaning products in sensitive areas can wreak all kinds of havoc with your electrical system.

The fiberglass fender panels behind the rear wheels can be easily removed to gain access to the engine. Cleaning the hundreds of aluminum fins, fittings and driveline parts will keep you delightfully engaged for many, many hours.

The 308's engine can be cleaned like any other aluminum engine. There are numerous products available that will work at cleaning and degreasing your engine. Be sure to get only aluminum safe detergents and follow the directions included. A detailing brush may be needed to get to some of the hard to reach spots, but for the most part, special equipment is not needed.

GTS Top

If you own a GTS 308, you're going to want to keep the black top clean. The top is made of fiberglass and painted black. Keeping the top looking new and glossy isn't difficult if you use a product specifically for fiberglass and paint. Car soap gets it clean, but doesn't bring out the glossy look. Wax shouldn't be used, and other protective cleaners just don't make it look right because they have a tendency to streak. The best products for your top are the ones designed for exterior rubber or fiberglass. As with all cleaning products, make sure to test it in an inconspicuous spot first, before applying the product to the rest of the area to be cleaned.

Scheduled Maintenance

With each new Ferrari 308, the factory included a warranty card and owner's service book. The service book lists each of the service intervals and which checks and procedures should be done at each service. The regular service intervals are approximately every 3000 miles, with the more in-depth minor service procedures every other 15,000 miles. Finally, there is a major service that must be completed every 30,000 miles.

Regular Services

The 3,000 mile services include all the basic checks and fluid replacements. Air and fuel filters are checked and the oil and oil filter are changed. It is your basic engine check up. The price for a regular service on a 308 is only a little more than an average vehicle.

It is important that you don't miss the 3,000 mile services. In addition to keeping your car running smoothly, they can catch any small problems before they get larger (and more expensive).

Minor service

The minor service is performed approximately every 15,000 miles and includes everything that a regular service includes as well as valve adjustments, alternator and air conditioning belt replacements, and safety inspection. Due to the valve adjustment, belt replacements and other inspections, the price of a minor service can approach $1,000 or more.

Major service

The major service should be done at least every 30,000 miles and is nearly a complete check-up for your 308. It includes inspection of practically every system on the car, lubrication of most parts, and replacement of parts, if necessary. There are also several belts and hoses that are replaced, even if they look acceptable, as a precautionary measure. Due to the extensive nature of a major service, the prices can easily exceed $3,000, while your car may be tied up for weeks.

The most important part replaced during a major service is the timing belts. These should be replaced at the minor services if your drive your vehicle with exuberance. Unlike many other engines, which have a belt life of up to 100,000 miles, the Ferrari engine places a great deal of stress on the belt material. Therefore, the recommended change interval is 15,000 miles or five years.

DOING IT YOURSELF

There is a lot of misconception about the difficulty of working on a Ferrari. Though this is true for some of the models (namely, the early 12-cylinder cars and all the newer models), the 308s are actually easy to work on for the average "do-it-yourselfer." Note, that this isn't an endorsement for you to do all the work on your car by yourself.

The difficulty of working on your 308 isn't the major concern. The biggest problem with doing the work yourself is that if you do it incorrectly, it will cost you a lot more money to fix your mistake. For example, something as common as an incorrect tension on the timing belt can cost you up to $10,000 in repair bills!

With that warning said, many of the DIY projects on a 308 aren't any different than other sports cars from the 70's and 80's. Regular maintenance and simple repairs can be done without difficulty. Just make sure you know what you're doing before you do it, and also be aware of the issues you can have (special tools, possible glitches, etc.).

The online communities and local owner's clubs can be a tremendous help when you're knee deep in a procedure and get stuck. They can also help you with tips and tricks on making most procedures easier. And, once you've completed a procedure correctly, you can proudly help others that are attempting it for the first time.

COMMON MAINTENANCE ITEMS

Before we embark upon what you can do, let's list what common items can be purchased for your 308 at the local auto parts store. In most cases there is no need to find an authorized Ferrari dealer and buy these items packaged in the expensive yellow and black boxes. All of the items below can be found in auto parts stores.

However, in most cases, you must be able to specify what you want by product, as very few computers or parts books have listings for Ferraris. And if your car is not in the auto parts store's computer, you simply don't exist. We don't list prices as they vary widely.

Lights

Every type of light on a 308 is standard and can be found anywhere. The key is knowing the standard number used by a majority of US manufacturers such as Wagner.

Headlights	H6024
Signal Lights	10732
Brake Lights	1034
Parking Lights	1034
Sidemarker Lights	194 (superseded the 158)
Dash lights	2723 and 17131 (or 3893)
License	67

Fuses and Relays

The fuses are out of an old VW, relays are simple Bosch type, and you need to cross-reference to standard if you don't want to pay the Bosch prices for relays. There are three operational types of relays in the 308. Once you have figured out the operation and configuration, you can find better and cheaper relays than Bosch. Try to always have on hand at least two or three relays as they control the windows, fuel pump, and other very critical circuits. A bad relay can and will leave you stranded.

Spark plugs

Champion, Autolite, and AC make good plugs available anywhere. Champion NY8 is recommended by the owners manual for 308 Carbureted, N6GY for 4 valve, or Bosch W 6 DS.

Belts

Belts will vary from model to model and from year to year. Usually you get the belt number from the old belt if it is still visible. If not, take it into the store and have them measure it. In most cases you will be able to find a direct, properly fitting replacement belt for the air conditioner, water pump, and alternator.

Windshield Wipers

Wipers can be purchased in refills, the blade only, or you can buy the blade and supporting structure as one unit. Anco lists the 25 series and the 31 type blade arms for the 308. In either event, you can walk into almost any auto parts store and purchase a new refill, or complete blade. Bring in your old one to match up for both length and type.

Hoses and clamps

There are no special molded hoses on the water system of a 308. All hoses are straight, in metric diameters, but SAE sizes will do in almost every case. They must be cut to fit, but are usually very inexpensive. We recommend replacing all the original Italian type clamps with good, stainless steel screw type hose clamps.

Oil Filter

There is a very important caveat here. As the oil filter sits upside down, it is of a special design to allow some oil to remain in the filter after the car is shutdown. The AC filter number is PF 2149, and given that number, you can cross reference to any other manufacturer. Double check to make sure the cross-referenced product has the special pipe design!

Fuel Filter

AC number is GF527, and used in the US version. Euro versions use a slightly different filter which has different threading.

Air Filter

No general listing here, but K&N offers a replacement filter which can be cleaned. Part number is 33-2019 for 1980 and up 308s.

Oil

Synthetic oils weren't widely available in the day of the 308s, but are widely regarded as the best oil to use in almost any case. Mobil 1 20W50 is a good choice, but watch your geographic location and make sure you are obtaining the correct viscosity for your region. The manual lists 10W50 AGIP oil, so use that as a guide. You many not want a 50 weight oil if you live in cold areas.

Brake Fluid

DOT 5 can be found in synthetic only—DOT 4 Castrol is good however. The owner's manual calls for DOT 3.

Anti Freeze

There are a number of new anti freeze products on the market today, including a variety which will not kill animals if swallowed. You must use aluminum safe antifreeze, and any good product designed for aluminum engines to protect against corrosion will work fine.

MAINTENANCE PROCEDURES

Now, as a proud owner, you may want to venture into performing some maintenance items by yourself, or with minimal help from your mechanic. There are some procedures that even novice do-it-yourselfers can perform without too much risk to your car.

Oil and Filter Change
An oil and oil filter change is one of the most basic maintenance jobs you can do on your own car. Although it can be messy, the procedure is not difficult and is not different than any other car. If you check your work, the danger is minimal.

The most important thing to be aware of is simply the large quantity of oil that will come out of the engine. You should have at least a 12-15 quart container to hold all of the oil. When you remove the oil drain plug it will come out—FAST. The oil should be warm when removed. You must also be careful with the drain bolt and the oil pan. Because the oil pan is aluminum, it is easy to accidentally strip the threads on the oil pan by trying to over-tighten the drain plug. Do not over-tighten the drain plug!

When removing the filter, pack rags around the filter to limit how much oil is spilled on your engine. Remember to always replace the filter with the correct type—the filters can not be identified merely by the size or shape. An incorrect oil filter without an internal pipe to hold oil back will appear the same and fit the same as the correct filter, so be warned. The factory recommends using 10w50 viscosity oil from Agip. It is not difficult to find oil in this range, but you can substitute it with 20W50. If you change to synthetic, change the filter and the drain all the old oil.

Changing Spark Plugs
Like the oil drain plug, the spark plugs are threaded into aluminum heads and the spark plug well-hole is very deep. Therefore it is very easy to cross thread the spark plugs, destroying the threads in the aluminum head. Again, a very important item to consider, be very careful when installing spark plugs!

Use a socket with a good rubber insert to grip the plugs as they are removed. The plugs on the front bank can be accessed by carefully extending your arm and wrench between the open engine lid and the rear window. If you have Popeye-shaped forearms this may be a problem.

Use a bit of oil or anti-seize on the new plugs before inserting. THREAD BY HAND until you are certain that the plug is threading correctly. Tighten but do not over-tighten. Use a torque wrench if in doubt!!

Brakes
The brakes on your 308 are hydraulically activated ventilated disc brakes. The front and rear brakes have separate hydraulic systems for redundancy in case one goes out. The brake system is vacuum assisted. The dashboard warning light will light when the emergency (hand) brake is on, or when there is a hydraulic problem in either the front or the rear braking system.

If you feel any vibration or notice a reduction in braking ability, you'll need to investigate. Problems could be as result of air or moisture in the braking system, a scored or warped disc, or worn pads. Ferrari recommends Ferodo I/D 332 and Ferodo I/D 346GG brake pads. There are several aftermarket manufacturers of standard and performance brake pads that fit the 308.

Changing the front brakes in a Ferrari 308 is similar to changing brakes in all other cars with hydraulic disc brakes. The rear brakes have a screw type system which withdraws the pistons and allows space to insert the new pads. If you're unsure of your ability to perform work on the brakes, take it to a mechanic.

Brake Fluid
You should check the brake fluid every month or two. This should be done without taking the lid off the reservoir. As long as the fluid level is between the "Min" and "Max" marks, it's in good shape.

Ferrari originally recommended Super HD DOT 3 brake fluid. If you want to use DOT 4 instead, it is an acceptable replacement. Using DOT 5 as a replacement is not recommended because it is composed of silicon, while DOT 3 and 4 are glycol based.

Due to moisture and contaminants, brake fluid should be replaced at least once every year, and more often if you drive with energy. If you notice you're low on brake fluid, instead of topping off the reservoir, flush the entire brake system and re-fill with new brake fluid. Another major warning here: brake fluid is fatal to the finish of your Ferrari!! NEVER get brake fluid on any painted surface. It will lift paint almost immediately! Take care when bleeding the brakes and replacing the brake fluid in the brake reservoir.

Carburetor
There are, no doubt, many readers of this book who are capable of mastering the art of maintaining multiple carburetion. It is almost a lost art, as the vast multitude of cars today use fuel injection and have done so for almost 20 years. A generation

has passed, and today's mechanics are simply not familiar with even so much as a two barrel Solex, much less a multiple Weber equipped V-8 Ferrari. However, carburetors are not mysterious nor is working on them a black art. If you are so inclined, have good manual dexterity, a sense of wind and noise, like to work over hot engines for hours, and are willing to spend good money on books, tools and special equipment, you may find working on Ferrari carbureted cars just your thing. If you hate model building, find it difficult to change light bulbs and wipers, or have someone else do your taxes, leave carburetor maintenance and tuning to an expert, provided you can find one.

If you have a carbureted Ferrari and are not an expert, just remember the basics:

1. Jetting, as provided by the factory with standard options for emissions, is correct. So long as you don't remove the air pump or make any other changes to the induction system, jetting should never change. Jets will get dirty and need cleaning, but rarely, if ever, need replacement. But I'd guess that many carburetor equipped 308s have had the air pump removed or disabled, or other changes made which will affect jetting, such as different camshafts. Therein lies the problem. Also, if you live in high altitude areas (such as Denver Colorado), you may have jet settings different than stock due to different atmospheric pressure at the high altitudes.

2. Once properly jetted, and the carburetors are synchronized properly with secure settings on all linkages, the Webers will rarely go 'out of tune'. Unless the linkages are wearing or the idle screws decide to go south, nothing should cause the carburetor settings to be upset. It is usually plugs, points, or other problems in the fuel system, such as the fuel itself or fuel pressure. Always ensure EVERYTHING ELSE is in proper condition before assuming problems are related to carburetion.

Tires

Tires are extremely important to your car's driving and handling its characteristics. They are your car's only contact with the road. In the 20 to 30 years since the 308 was released, tire technology has improved steadily. Tires available today are much more advanced than what was available then. By today's standards even the wheels are small and heavy.

If you have the stock wheels, there are quite a few choices when searching for tires. To help you decide which tires, here are the original wheel and tire sizes that came with the 308 series:

	Front Wheel	Front Tire	Rear Wheel	Rear Tire
GT4	6.5Jx14	205/70VR14	6.5Jx14	205/70VR14
GT4 (optional)	7Jx14	205/70VR14	7Jx14	205/70VR14
GTB/GTS	6.5Jx14	205/70VR14	6.5Jx14	205/70VR14
GTB/GTS opt.	7.5Jx14	205/70VR14	7.5Jx14	205/70VR14
GTBi/GTSi	165mmx390mm	240/55VR15	165mmx390mm	240/55VR15
GTBi/GTSi opt	6.5Jx14	205/70VR14	7.5Jx14	205/70VR14
QV	165mmx390mm	240/55VR15	165mmx390mm	240/55VR15
QV (optional)	7Jx16	205/55VR16	8Jx16	225/50VR16

If you're unlucky enough to have the metric rims (size 390mm), you may have difficulty finding a quality tire at any price below outrageous. Many owners of the metric rims have switched to the 7x16 and 8x16 rims just to get a selection of affordable tires.

COMMON PROBLEMS

In the following section I list some of the most common problems that a Ferrari 308 owner may encounter during their ownership. The listed problems aren't the only ones you'll ever see, and if you don't see many of them, consider yourself lucky. I've also attempted to include information on how to repair or at least deal with the problems. There are always multiple ways to deal with a problem, so if you've got a better solution, or your problem is slightly different, feel free to try something other than what's described here.

Oil Leaks
How do you know when your 308 is out of oil?

It stops leaking.

Although this joke goes for just about any exotic car, it is very true for 308's. There are many potential areas for leaks and because some of the gaskets in your engine are at least 20 years old, they're likely to be dried out or leaking at least a little. Cam seals and distributor seals are the most common and can be fixed relatively easily. You should have your leaks checked out right away. Leaking oil can contaminate many other parts of the engine and cause catastrophic problems. Oil can easily get "dripped" on the timing belt or alternator - neither of which is ever good. If you're not an experienced do-it-yourselfer, have a professional mechanic repair the problem as soon as possible.

Timing Belt

There's a great deal of debate on the topic of timing belts. Because the failure of this single piece can be so expensive, it deserves the attention it gets. Because the 308 engine is an "interference engine", any failure of valve timing will cause the pistons and valves to intersect the same space at the same time - causing a collision that results in damaging both. This kind of failure can easily cost $10,000 to repair.

Timing belts fail for any number of reasons. Often they break apart due to wear or oil contamination, or one of the notches on the belt can break off causing the timing to change, or the belt can slip due to improper tension. The factory recommends replacing the belts at the 30,000 mile services. Most owners have been successful with this interval, and if the engine is properly maintained (no leaks onto the belts or bearing failure) the belts can easily last this long. There is also a time limit on the belts because some Ferraris aren't driven often enough to make 30,000 miles. If after 5 years you haven't driven 30,000 miles it's advised to change the belts anyway.

If you wonder why the Honda can go 90,000 miles on a timing belt made of the exact same material as a Ferrari timing belt, bear in mind that the stress on the belts, the rpm, and the length and pressure on the belts has a great deal to do with the longevity of a belt. If you've changed the belts on both a Honda four and a Ferrari V-8 it becomes very easy to understand why the mileage requirements are so different.

Many wonder if it's beneficial to change the belt at 15,000 miles. Many people believe that it's cheap insurance to change the belts at the minor services. Although it adds to the price of the minor service, it's not a bad idea to keep the timing belt as fresh as possible. After all, the belts themselves still cost under $100, and if no other work is required, it is a fairly simple operation.

A full service change of belts and seals will be costly, however. The kicker is that once you have to remove the cam covers, a step necessary to lock the camshafts in place, you have already spent $100 on the gaskets. Once opened up, why not check the cam shims for correct settings? And, of course while you are at it, replace the camshaft seals with the updated versions which won't leak as often. All that can be done on one new set of $100 paper cam cover gaskets.

Getting 2nd Gear

This is one of the most common issues for 308 owners. Until the transmission is thoroughly warmed up, getting into second gear smoothly and quickly is darn near impossible. The solution is to make sure the transmission is warmed up, and if you're still having problems try using a high quality synthetic gear oil in your transmission. This helps in most cases.

The Clock

What do you need to know the time for anyway? Actually, the clock is one of the most common failures in 308s. In addition to the mechanical parts wearing (not being able to adjust the time), the clear plastic lens often gets scratched and yellowed. There are replacements available, and if yours is broken, it's not difficult to replace it completely or send it out for repairs. There are several repair shops around the country that you can send your original clock to for rejuvenation. They will repair it and send it back to you in excellent condition. The cost of the repairs is usually under $200.

Slow Windows

Slow power windows on one or both sides of the 308 are a very common problem. Sometimes they're slow at just the bottom or the top, and sometimes they're slow all the way up. Luckily there are several possible fixes to the problem, and one or more of them can help greatly in their speed.

The electric motors for the power windows require a large amount of current. Any corrosion on the contacts or leads in the electronic circuit will decrease the current getting to the motor and thereby reduce the power of the motors. Dried out rubber and trim add to the problem by requiring much more resistance than originally planned. Additionally, the entire mechanical system and strength of the motors barely meets the requirements.

To repair the problem you should first try adding some lubrication to the rubber and trim that is in contact with the window glass as it moves up and down. Making the movement easier will help no matter what the cause. If this clears up the problem completely, consider yourself lucky and call it a day. If not, try cleaning all the contacts at all parts of the electrical system. The contacts are at several points in the circuit, including between the fuse block and the switch and between the switch and the motor. You'll have to remove the interior door panel to gain access to some of the contacts. Make sure the contacts inside the switch are not corroded as well. Using fine sand-paper, steel wool or a nail file, clean the contacts to make sure the bare metal is exposed and will make proper contact when connected. When making the connections, you can also include an anti-oxidant dielectric grease to help maintain the integrity of the connection for longer periods of time.

If these attempts don't fix the problem, you may be forced to do the last dramatic repair. You may have to take the whole mechanical system apart and re-assemble it after lubricating the parts. This is not for the faint of heart, as the system is fairly complex with a variety of wires, pulleys, and motors.

Poor Gauge Lighting

If you've driven your 308 at night with the lights on, you've noticed that the luminosity of the gauge lights is minimal at best. To increase the brightness you have to install new bulbs in the dash. There are four bulbs in the instrument cluster, two smaller bulbs, and two medium-sized bulbs. The sizes are Sylvania #2723 and #3893. Opening the instrument cluster and installing these bulbs makes a big difference.

However, if you upgrade your lights and they still aren't bright enough, you may have a problem with your dimmer switch. The switch is a variable resistor and has possibly deteriorated during the 20 years since it was installed. If it is your dimmer switch, you have two possible solutions. First, you can bypass the dimmer switch completely. Your lights will be at full brightness, but that usually isn't bad. Secondly, you can replace the dimmer switch completely by finding the replacement part.

Fuel Injection

With the stock system, there isn't a lot you can do other than make sure the injection jets are clean. Regularly using fuel additives that clean fuel injectors is advised in most cases. If the fuel additives don't work, you can have them professionally cleaned at any number of repair shops.

Dead Battery

As we have stated, trickle chargers are a necessary option for any car that sits for long periods of time.

These can be purchased for a relatively small amount (less than a new battery) from any number of stores. The 308 uses a standard 12-volt automotive battery, so there doesn't have to be anything special about the charger.

CV Boot

The constant velocity (CV) joints on the rear axles of the 308 are not a weak point on the car, but the CV boots are another story. There are 4 boots, 2 on each axle and they are made of a rubber material that wasn't meant to last 20 years. When the boots get old and cracked they let the grease escape, no longer providing lubrication to the axles and they let dirt and debris into the joint area. Replacing a damaged boot at early signs of degradation can save you from having to purchase an entire CV joint.

The process of replacing the boot is not difficult except for one part - removing the bolts that hold the axle in place. To remove these you'll need the correct size metric wrench, a large breaker bar, and probably a long pipe to break it free. Once the bolt is off, changing the grease and boots is not difficult. You do not need any special grease to re-pack the joints.

Rear Trunk Cover & Zipper

This is an extremely common problem with the older cars. As the trunk temperature fluctuates from cold to hot and back to cold again, the leather becomes less pliable, and shrinks, causing the weak point (the zipper) to split. Replacing the zipper slider is about your only simple solution. If replacing the slider doesn't fix the problem, you may have to replace either the entire zipper or the entire cover if it has shrunk too much.

Hoses

After many years of operation or sitting, even the best quality hoses will deteriorate. Generally, hoses tend to deteriorate from the inside outward, so checking the current condition by looking at the outside of a hose does not give the most accurate results. You can try squeezing the hoses to get a general guess as to the condition, but it's still just guesswork.

If you're unsure of the last time hoses were changed, you may want to consider replacing them. Having them go out while driving can be very messy and may result in a ruined engine. The oil, coolant, and fuel hoses should all be replaced if they're original, or of unknown age. Replace them with high-quality hoses that can handle the pressures involved and use high-quality, new hose clamps.

CHAPTER 7

Performance, Tuning, and Mods

MODIFYING YOUR 308

You've owned your 308 for what, three days? And now you're wondering what you can do to the car to make it faster, smoother, and more unique. Although most die hard Ferraristi frown on such things, there are some cases where modifying and updating your 308 can be a positive thing.

Whenever you're going to enhance or modify something on your car, there will be some negative consequences; otherwise, the factory would have done it. The upside of a modification can be increased horsepower, torque, handling, braking, and more. While the downsides can range from cost (in both cost of the upgrade and lowering the resale value) to decreased engine life expectancy (increased wear and tear).

You may wonder why the most die-hard Ferrari enthusiast is so disdainful of any changes, even those that actually improve the car. One reason is because traditionally, Ferrari owners have gone to great lengths and expense to bring their cars back to original condition (never mind that they are often in the wrong color and ten times cleaner and shinier than when they left the factory!). The special concours d'elegance events held during Ferrari club events and specials shows at Palm Beach and Monterey hold originality in extremely high regard. Ferraris that have been modified in any way are put into a special class.

Eventually, either you or the next owner (remember you are but a caretaker) may want to enter a concours. So, before you perform any modification, weigh the pros and cons carefully. Make sure the desired results are the ones you really want, and that you're willing to accept the consequences.

LEARNING TO DRIVE CORRECTLY

By far, the largest single thing you can do to increase your 308's performance is learn to drive it correctly. By learning how to use all of your Ferrari's capabilities, the perceived performance gain is quite staggering. In addition, as a more skilled driver, when you make mechanical modifications to the car, you can better evaluate the differences the changes make, as well as utilize them to the most benefit. As the old saying goes: the first nut to change is the one behind the steering wheel.

The upside of learning to drive correctly includes increasing your driving knowledge, how to handle extreme situations, the ability to avoid accidents, and a proper respect for the design and engineering by Ferrari engineers. Learning to drive correctly and safely can save your life. The only major downside to this "upgrade" is the cost of any schools, as well as the time you must invest.

But You Already Know How to Drive
Yes, it's true. You probably do know how to drive, according to the laws and driving principles you were taught in high school. But, you're not driving your mother's mini-van anymore. You are driving a high performance exotic sports car that can break those laws without working up a sweat. The techniques of driving a 308 are completely different from most other road going cars. Remember it is a very low, mid-engine, rear wheel drive, high performance sports car utilizing technology which is already over a quarter of a century old. That's a potent combination!

The best way to increase your driving skill is to learn how to drive safely in your new 308, and then learn how to drive it faster.

Safety First
First, we must include a warning statement:
Exceeding the posted speed limit and driving as if the public streets are a race track is very dangerous. Not only is it against the law, but it can get you and innocent people injured or killed. Think of the possible consequences before you act, and obey all traffic laws.

The next thing to remember when driving your Ferrari is that it is small. Very small. In fact, it's so low that most SUV's can't see you when you're right behind them. You could be right behind them honking your horn and screaming, while you watch them put it into reverse and back right into your hood. (I know from personal experience that this can and does happen!) Try to remember that you'll get a lot of gawkers looking at the car, but you'll also get a lot of drivers that won't even know there was a car near them. Keep this in mind when passing or tailgating another driver. Avoid tailgating and stay out of other driver's blind spots. And always check your blind spot before turning or changing lanes. Many gawkers drive in your blind spot to get a better look, not realizing they're in your blind spot.

Next, keep a vigilant watch for bumps, inclines, or other obstacles that may run into your front valence. Although especially true for those of you with a Euro front spoiler, even the US versions are low. The best way to avoid scraping or cracking your valence is to take inclines very slowly and at an angle - don't take them straight on. By making one tire take the incline or bump first, you can reduce the angle between the incline and the lower portion of your car.

Other pitfalls are curbs and potholes. Even small potholes and bumps can ruin those nice alloy rims. Curbs can also be dangerous, so become familiar with the width of your 308. I'm not recommending those little "feeler" attachments, but I am suggesting that you be careful around curbs and rough roads. The rims aren't cheap, and the OEM wheels are becoming harder to find.

And finally, a word about "street racing" or "drag racing". The 308 isn't a muscle car, and it wasn't made for burn-outs or straight line racing. It was made for road racing, with an emphasis on handling and style. Though its horsepower and torque are great, it won't compare with many of the modified imports cruising the street. Your 308 is over 20 years old -even though it doesn't look like it. And just because the label says "Ferrari" does not mean that it is particularly fast!

Driving your 308
As you already know, the 308 is unlike any other car you've ever driven. It is a mid-engine sports car with rear-wheel drive. During normal driving these factors won't become apparent, but when the car is pushed, these properties will start to make a noticeable difference. If you're not prepared for these differences, you can be caught off guard, and end up with your car against a curb.

Driving Position
To "feel" a 308 correctly (and to drive it comfortably), you must be in a relaxed and correct seating position. Your head should not be smashed against the roof, your legs should not be reaching for the pedals, and your arms should not be stretched out.

First, adjust the lateral position of the seat. In the 308's stock seats, the adjustment lever is located at the front of the seat on the right side. Push down on the lever and move the seat forward or backward so that your feet can reach the pedals. Your left foot should be able to press the clutch pedal all the way to the floor without extending your leg completely. Next, adjust the seat-back angle to allow your arms to easily reach the steering wheel and be able to turn it without moving your back off the seat. You should be able to easily reach the gear shifter without stretching. Also, if your head is touching the roof, you may have to set the seat at a larger incline than you are used to. The knob for seat-back angle adjustment is on the outside of the seat where the seat bends. You should have support on your upper legs all the way up to your upper back.

Once you are seated comfortably, adjust your mirrors to match your new position. Adjustment of the center rear view mirror is fairly simple, as the rear window is not that large. Adjust it so that you can see directly behind you as much as possible. The driver and passenger side rear view mirrors should be adjusted to allow you to see the lanes next to you.

If your seat is set up correctly, you should be able to sit and drive like that for several hours at a stretch without discomfort. You may have to adjust slightly each time you drive, but it's entirely a personal preference. You should be able to feel your 308 AND be comfortable.

Mid-engine Handling
The 308 engine is placed directly in front of the rear tires, with the transmission also at the rear of the car. This makes the weight balance of the car almost neutral - split equally between the front and rear tires. The 308 also has a small "moment of inertia" because most of the weight is in the same general area. These factors make the car react very quickly to steering, but also make it feel a bit twitchy at the limit.

High Performance Driving
High performance driving is a learned skill. It's not something people are born with. It requires learning the basics, practicing the techniques, and using your knowledge correctly. If you really want to drive your 308 at the limit, you must go to a local track or an autocross event. These are the only places that you can safely put your car through a workout without breaking the law or putting others in danger.

Schools
There are dozens of reputable driving schools out there, and the best way to start is to find one that fits your goals and budget. The schools can be expensive, so read

as much about them as you can before you make a decision to attend. Ask online or get referrals from friends. If you're new to performance driving, you should start with a school that uses street-legal (or "almost street legal") vehicles and treaded tires. This can give you a better introduction because the instructors can ride with you and give you real-time feedback on your driving technique.

Generally, all schools can be broken down into one of three categories: Defensive Driving, Road Racing, and Formula Racing. Most schools will emphasize one of the above categories as well as have some training in the other areas.

The defensive driving courses focus on handling various situations that you could run into on the street. They focus on things like wet weather driving, accident avoidance, passing, emergency braking, and "safe zone" principles. Be careful though, as some schools are just for people that are trying to get out of a ticket. Still others focus on "Corporate Drivers" for body guards and executives with enemies.

Road racing schools are probably the best place to start. Typically the first day is spent learning the basic principles of racing including gear changes, turning, and braking. Then they move on to road racing skills including trail braking, cornering lines, and passing. You learn how cars behave and react at the limit.

Formula racing schools are just like the name implies. You will drive an open wheel formula racecar around a track. They teach similar knowledge and techniques just like the road racing schools, but the cars are lighter, faster, and quicker around the track. Because the cars are so different, your technique and skill must be slightly more advanced. It's a real thrill to go around a race track in an open wheeled formula racer. Some even offer multi-day classes that start in a normal street car, and then advance to the open wheel cars. The down side to this type of program is the price, which is usually several thousand dollars.

AUTOMOTIVE AND RACING CLUBS

There are many national and regional clubs that focus on automobile ownership, racing, and Ferraris. If you want to get started in racing or concours d'elegance competitions, check out these clubs. Membership fees are usually under $100/year and are nearly always worth the money.

SCCA
The Sports Car Club of America (SCCA) is a club dedicated to racing and rallying sports cars. The SCCA is a national organization with 110 regional chapters, over 2,000 motor sports events each year, and over 60,000 members. With the help of

volunteers and members, they organize racing events of all varieties, including Solo I (time trial), Solo II (autocross), driver education, rallies, and pro racing.

The SCCA is not specific to Ferraris, and this makes it a great place to find owners of other exotic and unusual cars. If you live in an active region, the SCCA can have events near you nearly every weekend throughout the year. You can contact the SCCA through their website at http://www.scca.org or by calling 1-800-770-2055. They can sign you up and direct you to your local chapter.

FCA

The Ferrari Club of America (FCA) is "the Club for Ferrari People" and is dedicated entirely to Ferrari owners and enthusiasts. With nearly 5,000 members, the FCA is divided into several large regions throughout the United States and Canada. Dues are currently around $100 per year ($135 in most states), and with the dues you also get a monthly club newsletter.

Numerous FCA events are held throughout the country. Events range from simple get-togethers and car shows, to full out racing events, time trials, and fun rallies. It's a great place to meet other Ferrari owners and Ferraristi. You can contact the FCA through their website at http://www.ferrariclubofamerica.com/ or by calling them at 1-800-328-0444.

FOC

The Ferrari Owner's Club (FOC) is similar to the FCA and was established in 1961. The FOC was the first Ferrari club authorized by the Ferrari factory. The club is not quite as large as the FCA, but the people are just as wonderful.

The FOC has particularly large and active chapters on the east and west coasts. They tend to focus more on racing events, but they also have all kinds of events including rallies, picnics and concours d'elegance. The price of membership is currently $105 per year with an additional $15 in some regions. Their website is available at http://www.ferrariownersclub.org/ and includes an online membership application.

Performance Events

If you want to try out some of the advanced characteristics and capabilities of your 308, there are a variety of speed events, from simple "educational" events all the way to heart pounding wheel-to-wheel racing.

Driver's Education

Driver's "Ed" events are not considered a "racing" event because your lap times are not recorded. They focus on getting the drivers out on the track and playing with their cars near the limits. The emphasis is placed on safety and learning the limits and abilities of the car and the driver.

While the events are not timed, and racing wheel to wheel is not permitted, there is a definite possibility of damaging or crashing your vehicle. Whenever you are traveling around a race course at high speed and near the limit there is a possibility of losing control and damaging your 308. Some insurance providers consider these events to be "racing" or "performance" driving events, and will not cover the vehicle in the event of an accident. You should verify that you are covered by reviewing your policy.

Autocross/Solo II
Autocrosses are the safest form of "timed" or racing event because they take place in large open areas of asphalt or concrete. These are usually in large parking lots or similar open spaces with lots of pavement. Most clubs that sanction events require a maximum speed limit (usually around 60mph) as well as ample run-off for missed corners.

Even though this is one of the safest forms of racing, the increased possibility for damage still exists. Most issues arrive from pushing the car and driver to the limits and causing internal mechanic problems including missed shifts, overheating, and suspension failures.

If you're interested in starting in any type of motor sports, autocrosses are a great place to begin your training.

TimeTrials/Solo I
Much like a driver's education event, these often take place on a race track or closed course (such as a hill climb), but have the limitation of one vehicle in any area at a time. This prevents the wheel-to-wheel contact that can get very expensive.

Solo I racing is more dangerous than driver's education and autocross events because it is a racing situation with limited run off room and higher speeds. They are usually not recommended for inexperienced drivers.

Racing (Wheel-to-wheel) Events
For the braver, and necessarily better funded 308 owners, the possibility of racing wheel to wheel against other racers is a definite thrill. Racing can be very dangerous to your car, especially for the exterior. Damage to the engine and suspension wear could incur fairly substantial costs. Starting in wheel-to-wheel almost always requires installation of a roll cage, fire extinguisher(s), tow connection, an external shut-off switch, and a special racing license. You shouldn't

even consider racing wheel to wheel until you're an excellent race driver and have earned a racing license from an approved organization.

ENGINE PERFORMANCE

Now that you know what you're doing, you can start looking at improving the performance of the 308. The V-8 is a strong performer right out of the box, but as technology changes, there are many new things available to increase the power produced by your engine.

One of the ways to think about the performance of an engine is to think of it as an "air pump." In general, the better an engine can breathe its air-fuel mixture, the more power it can generate. So, by allowing the engine to breathe both more and easier, you will be able to generate more power.

Note that combinations of different modifications might be detrimental to each other, so careful planning is important. If you're going to make a lot of modifications it might be beneficial to have dyno tests done to determine the performance of your car after every few changes. This will help you determine what is helping, and by how much. It will also show you if there are any problems or detrimental combinations.

Air Filters
One of the few things that changed between the 308 models, at least slightly, is the air filter configuration. Air filters are necessary to keep foreign debris from entering your engine. Without an air filter, the dust sucked in through your engine would cause tremendous additional friction, reducing its useful lifetime to only a few thousand miles. Depending on how much wear you're willing to accept, you can increase the air flow through your engine by reducing the amount of filtering. Changing the air filter to one that allows more air through with less restriction allows the engine to breathe easier.

There are several manufacturers of high performance air filters, and versions are available for all models of the 308. In addition to simple filters, a few manufacturers also produce completely different intake paths.

Headers

There were two versions of the 308 headers, one for the US market and one for the European market. You can increase the air flow rate through the engine by upgrading to high performance headers. Tubi makes a high performance header that can increase your power by a small amount. Coating your current headers with thermally enhanced surfaces may also improve the performance slightly.

Muffler

The primary purpose of your muffler is to limit the amount of exhaust noise emitted from your engine. Unfortunately as part of that noise cancellation, there is a small amount of performance decrease due to the restricted airflow. Ferrari mufflers are excellent right from the factory, but their goal was to make most of their customers happy with the amount of noise coming from the rear of the car. Aftermarket producers of performance mufflers are more concerned with power than with noise. They want you to have more power and, if possible, sound better.

So, the trade off that you make for more power is a louder exhaust note. This is not necessarily a bad thing, since it is a Ferrari, but it does change the exhaust note slightly. There are several producers of excellent mufflers for the 308, including Ansa, Stebro, Capristo, and Tubi. Your choice for which muffler to put on your 308 will mostly depend on your budget. Don't expect to gain too much power though, as usually not more than a few horsepower is lost in the muffler.

Test Pipe

The so called "test pipe" is a straight through exhaust tube that completely replaces the catalytic converters in your exhaust path. It is called a "test pipe" because it is illegal to remove your catalytic converters and drive these cars on the street. You can use test pipes on a track car, or at the dyno shop, but driving a 308 with test pipes on the street is illegal and should never be done.

Catalytic converters reduce the airflow through the exhaust and also increase the amount of heat underneath the vehicle. By removing the "cats" you can increase power through less restricted air flow as well as less heat in the engine compartment. The down side of using test pipes (other than the legality issue) is that your emissions could increase, though there have been reports that a properly tuned car with test pipes installed can still pass some state emission tests.

An alternative to the full "test pipe" is to use high-flow performance catalytic converters. These allow your 308 to remain street legal while reducing the negatives associated with the catalytic converters. Varieties of performance converters are available from manufacturers such as HyperFlow and DynoMax.

NOS

Nitrous oxide can be enticing. It's almost like power for nothing and is often one of the least expensive upgrades to make, but the long term costs can be tremendous. Nitrous oxide (also known as "nos") adds power to the engine in a couple of ways. First, it provides more oxygen to the engine, increasing the amount of energy released in the combustion chamber. In addition to the increased oxygen, the nitrous oxide cools the air in the chamber, which allows even more air into the combustion chamber, creating additional power.

Nitrous oxide systems can add anywhere between 40 and 150 bhp to a 308 engine. But the extra power isn't completely free. Nitrous is extremely hard on the engine for two reasons. First, because more power is produced, the stress and wear on the internal components is significantly increased. Secondly, the nitrous can also substantially increase the heat generated inside the engine. Now that even the newest 308 engines are twenty years old, the added stress of nitrous oxide could easily turn a small mechanical issue to a major component failure.

Turbo/Superchargers

Turbochargers and superchargers help the engine make more power by forcing more air into the combustion chamber. Turbo systems accomplish this by using power from the exhaust to turn a turbine that pushes more air into the intake. Superchargers draw their power directly from the engine (usually via the crankshaft) to turn a compressor that pushes more air into the intake.

There are a few aftermarket kits that provide turbo and supercharger power for the 308. The kits increase the power by up to 200hp, and this power doesn't come without some serious side effects. Both systems work by dramatically increasing the air pressure in the combustion chamber. This is made even more dramatic when the piston compresses the air prior to detonation. The amount of stress and extra wear on engine parts is large. Although most people do not recommend using turbos or superchargers on your 308, it's a viable method for increasing the power of your engine. Kits and systems are available from a few sources, with the most notable being done by Norwood Autocraft out of Dallas, Texas.

SUSPENSION AND CHASSIS MODS

Tires

The range of tire choices available is huge and it changes every few months as tire manufacturers continuously release better and better tires. By now, the tires that originally came with your 308 are long gone; and that's a good thing. The tires available now are leaps and bounds above tires made just ten years ago.

The best way to determine which tires you should put on your 308 is to ask other 308 owners about the current "hot" tire. If you drive your car in the rain, you'll need a good all weather tire with excellent performance. If you never drive in the rain, you can look at serious high performance tires that don't handle that well in the rain. Really examine how you'll be using your 308 when determining which tires to purchase.

The perfect size tires for the 308 is always a matter of debate among 308 owners. The largest tires that fit on the 308 rims and under the fender, around a 245/45, will not greatly increase your traction, handling, or drivability but will increase your rolling resistance and un-sprung weight. Yet the stock tires may be just a little smaller than what the car can easily handle. A good size tire that increases handling capability while avoiding the needless increase in weight and rolling resistance is probably around a 225/50 on the front, and around 235/50 on the back. Of course, if you're using newer and larger wheels, a different tire may be more appropriate.

The minimum speed rating you should even consider is a V rated tire. H rated tires are available, but the 308 can go beyond the 130mph maximum of the H tires. Speed ratings of at least V, W, Y, or Z should only be used.

Wheels

The standard Ferrari wheels (also known as "rims") are great, but they are dated in both size and weight. Like tire technology, since the introduction of the 308, there have been many innovations in wheel technology. The original wheels still look great, but if you're upgrading your car and are limited by tire choices, you can safely find quality alternatives that fit. Most rims up to 17" will fit without any modification. Generally going to a 17" wheel can be done without a problem, and you can usually find more high performance tires in that size.

For a good combination of tire size and wheel size, you should work directly with the people supplying your wheels and tires. They'll have the best information on wheel offsets and acceptable sizes for the rims you are evaluating. The choices and designs are always changing, so keep an eye out for possibilities. And above all, remember what we said about originality. Under no conditions should you attempt to alter the body by flaring the fenders to fit wider tires. This could cost you a fortune down the road!

Brakes

Bigger brakes stop your car faster, and better brakes can make a huge difference in your lap times and handling. They can also improve the safety by allowing you to stop more confidently. If you have increased your tire size you can take advantage of your increased contact patch by installing one of the several available 308 brake upgrade kits. Additionally, larger rotors with pre-drilled holes can substantially reduce brake fading due to overheated hydraulic fluid, pads and rotors.

The brake kits usually include new calipers and rotors that are practically bolt-on replacements. The 308 does not have an Anti-lock braking system, which makes changing and modifying the brakes a relatively easy task. Check online or ask your local mechanic for manufacturers of brake kits.

Better brake pads are a common and easy upgrade that can be done when you're replacing the worn pads. New pads can increase stopping power and reduce the amount of brake dust around the wheels. The difference between pads can be noticeable. Brake pads designed for performance street use are a great improvement, but make sure to check the amount of noise and warm-up time they sometimes require.

Stainless steel brake lines are another common upgrade to the brake system. Unfortunately, they usually don't have any performance benefits, and can sometimes even make examination of the lines more tricky. Unless the braided stainless steel hoses are high quality, you could be setting yourself up for trouble. Use high quality OEM hoses and you won't be sorry - they won't look as nice, but when they're fatigued and bulging, you'll be able to see it and replace it.

Suspension

The stock suspension on all 308's is excellent. Even 20 years later it's still no slouch. With that being said, there are still many modifications that can improve the handling performance of your 308. The hardest part of suspension modifications is getting everything working together to achieve the desired result. Small changes in one area can ruin or overpower other changes. If you're making major changes to your suspension, plan on spending a lot of time fine-tuning the setup to meet your expectations.

Shocks wear out and may need rebuilding or replacing. They can be substituted with a number of different types of shock absorbers. Spending the extra money on adjustable shocks is often the correct thing to do if you know other suspension changes are in your future. Koni, Bilstein, and others make excellent replacement shock absorbers.

The stock 308 springs are large and at low, but easily manageable height. They aren't so stiff that every bump in the road will jerk your backside, and they're far from the lenient springs of most sport sedans. The advancements in metallurgy and springs isn't huge, but you can now purchase smaller and lighter springs that will perform at least as good, if not better than the stock springs. The smaller diameter springs can allow some larger wheels, while the weight savings improves overall suspension geometry and weight distribution. Shorter springs will lower the 308's ride height, but don't lower it too much more or you'll scrape the front valence constantly.

Bushings are another upgrade that can noticeably change the ride characteristics. Going straight to metal bushings might seem like a great idea at first, but beware - you'll hear and feel every crack in the road. A high quality urethane bushing will feel better and react better in almost every situation. The downside is that if they're not lubricated well with silicone lubricant, they may squeak rather loudly.

Anti-sway bars (also known as anti-roll bars or just sway bars) connect the left and right side of the suspension system using short lever ends to counteract body roll while cornering. There are several sizes available and most are fully adjustable, allowing for correct balancing for the front and rear suspension. More stiffness on the front anti-sway bar will produce more understeer (or "push"), while too much stiffness in the rear will cause the car to oversteer (or be "loose"). For most drivers, it's better to have a little more understeer until you're more familiar with driving a rear engine sports car.

MISCELLANEOUS UPGRADES

Stereo/Speakers
Let's face it - true Ferraristi would rather listen to the sweet 308 engine tones while driving rather than the radio. Within the first few hours of ownership of my second 308 (a GTS), I had completely disconnected the stereo, and removed most of the components. The only time I listen to anything other than the engine is on trips longer than an hour - it can be almost hypnotic for long drives. I'll also admit that while I'm not alone in this aversion to radios in Ferraris, most people prefer to have some type of music or entertainment in their car.

The most difficult part of replacing or upgrading the stereo in a 308 is the limited amount of space. There simply isn't room for additional components such as amplifiers or large subwoofers. The available space for the head unit is adequate, and will fit a huge variety of radios. There is almost no space in the doors for larger speakers. Possible locations will depend on which type of 308 you own.

Although it make take some custom work, a medium size subwoofer can fit in the passenger foot-well. On GTB and GTS models, additional speakers can be mounted on the panel in front of the rear window. And for GTB models, an amplifier can be mounted behind the driver or passenger seat. This can't be done on a GTS because the area is needed for roof storage.

Whatever stereo upgrades you choose to install, it is usually considered bad karma to make too many permanent modifications to your 308. Small holes and extra wiring are okay, but major amateur changes can definitely bring down the value of your car. High quality, professional upgrades are usually not frowned on as much.

Bits & Pieces
There are any number of different small custom pieces that aren't performance upgrades, but do add a little distinctiveness to your vehicle. Without over-customizing your car, you can add aluminum, carbon fiber, or titanium interior pieces to separate your car from other 308s. Whatever changes you do make, remember to keep the original parts packed away safely and securely.

The original gas cap on all 308s is a matte black while newer Ferrari caps are chrome, carbon fiber, or titanium. Most also have an engraved Cavallino Rampante. Several places online sell nice looking replacements. Though, you may be the only person that ever notices, since the cap is hidden under the louvers.

Another great small change is replacing the original black shift knob with an aluminum, stainless steel or carbon fiber. They just add a little flair to the inside of your vehicle and can make a subtle but noticeable difference. An even more subtle change is replacing the clutch, brake, and accelerator pedals with drilled aluminum pieces or covers. Try not to get the smooth pedals, as they will be very slippery when if your feet are wet.

Body Kits, Panels and Spoilers
Generally, because the 308 is a classic and its design is one of the greatest in automobile history, you don't want to mess around with its styling. Frankly, adding anything takes away from the overall balance of the car. The only time that changes won't take away from the looks (and therefore the value) is if your 308 body is damaged and must be replaced anyway.

There are several "factory" changes you can make to your 308, such as including the "buttress spoiler" that was an option on the later Quattrovalvoles. It's also possible to upgrade a U.S. version 308 to appear more like the European version by changing the front spoiler to the lower and deeper version, and changing the rear view mirrors to the black Euro style. Although most Ferraristi would choke at the idea, there are also body kits available that will make your 308 look like the hyper-aggressive 288 GTO. High quality kits will be expensive, and you will not get your money back when you sell the car.

Fire Extinguisher

A fire extinguisher is invaluable when you own a 308, and this is extremely true if your 308 is carbureted or is equipped with air-pumps and catalytic converters. The possible fuel leaks combined with the extremely high temperatures makes a volatile mix. If you're not convinced, just try searching online for burned out 308s. If you're prepared with a fire extinguisher, you can quickly limit the amount of damage caused by the rare, but possible, fire.

There are two main types of fire extinguishers. Chemical-based extinguishers, which are the usual household ones you can find at any hardware store, and Halon extinguishers, which are harder to come by and are more expensive compared to the chemical based ones. You do NOT want to use a chemical-based extinguisher anywhere near your 308. The chemicals will ruin most components and make a horrible mess. Halon is the only way to go.

Several sizes of Halon extinguishers are available. For most applications, a 2.5 pound extinguisher should be adequate. If your thoughts on the subject are "better safe than sorry", you can also fit a 5 pound extinguisher in the 308, but it does take up more space, and the mounting locations are limited.

The easiest place for mounting an extinguisher in the 308 is right in front of the passenger seat. The extinguisher will sit safely and out of the way, under the passenger's knees. A mounting bracket can be attached to the front bolts on the seat rails, and it won't require drilling any additional holes in the chassis. It also looks pretty cool, and makes grabbing it in a hurry much easier. Other mounting locations include behind the driver's seat (tight fit if you need your seat all the way back), and between the seats, mounted on the firewall - though any "behind-the-seat" mounting on a GTS will severely restrict stowing the top behind the seats.

Belts/Harness

Although there is nothing wrong with the seat belts included on your 308, there are certain times when you'd like a little more protection. There are a couple of different types of upgrades you can make to your seatbelts, with the most common being the addition of 4 and 5 point harnesses. The 4 point harnesses go across your lap, and also one belt over each shoulder. The 5 point harnesses have the same connections as the 4 point, but in addition, they have a "anti-submarine" belt which goes between the legs. This additional belt prevents you from sliding below the steering wheel, and keeps you in your seat better. These are probably not entirely useful on a 308, but if you're looking for more protection, it couldn't hurt. Mounting of new belts or harnesses should only be done by a professional. Belts are an integral part of the safety equipment, and improper mounting can cause more harm than just using the standard belts. You'll also need to check with your local Department of Motor Vehicles to see if any modifications require certification.

Roll Bar/Cage

This is a major "enhancement", and one that can't easily be undone. It can also severely reduce the resale value of your 308. But, if you are going to be racing your 308 on the track, it is highly recommended (and required in most wheel-to-wheel classes). Generally, you'll have to find a mechanic/welder/metal-worker to do the installation, since there are no real providers of "production" bars. Also, check the requirements of the racing class. There are usually very specific rules for what is and isn't allowed. The ID, OD, and thickness of the bars are almost always outlined in the regulations. Seek a professional installer before attempting to add a roll cage.

MORE INFORMATION

- Ferrari Tuning Tips & Maintenance Techniques by Gerald Roush & John Apen. This book was originally published in the 1970's, and it is now back in print and available through Veloce Press at www.VelocePress.com. It is also available through Amazon.com and used books come up on eBay occasionally.

- Ferrari Guide to Performance by Allen S. Bishop. A classic book on Ferrari performance upgrades. Although the book spends most time on V-12's, there is a section on V-8's and an interesting story of using NOS in a 308. This book is available from Veloce Press at www.VelocePress.com and used copies can be found online.

- Guy Croft WSM, Modifying & Tuning Fiat/Lancia Twin-cam Engines by Guy Croft, Motor Racing Publications. Although this book isn't technically for Ferraris, it has many procedures that can be used on the 308 engines.

- Online resources such as FerrariList.com and FerrariChat.com are invaluable when researching performance upgrades. Ask the online groups for their opinions about Ferrari topics, and you'll get plenty of answers

OTHER FERRARI BOOKS AVAILABLE FROM VELOCEPRESS

Ferrari Tuning Tips & Maintenance Techniques

Out-of-print and largely unavailable for years, Ferrari Tuning Tips & Maintenance Techniques was originally published by Jim Riff as Ferrari Tuning Tips & Techniques. Following two highly successful editions Gerald Roush and John Apen expanded and revised the work, which subsequently went through three printings from 1975 to 1977. Even though it has been nearly 25 years since its last revision, Ferrari Tuning Tips & Maintenance Techniques still contains essential information for the Ferrari enthusiast and mechanic.

Covers the: 250 GT, 250 GTE, 330 GT, 330 GTC, 365 GT, 365 GTB/4, 365 GTC/4, Dino 246 GT

Author: Gerald Roush and John Apen. **Pages:** 164. **Dimensions:** 8 1/4" x 11".

Ferrari Serial Numbers Part I

A revised and updated VelocePress edition of Hilary A. Raab Jr.'s "Ferrari Serial Numbers Part I" that covers all of the odd-numbered Ferraris (normally reserved for the Ferrari street cars) to serial number 21399. The companion title, "Ferrari Serial Numbers Part II", covers the even numbered chassis (racing cars) through serial number 1050.

Author: Hilary A. Raab. **Pages:** 224. **Dimensions:** 8 1/4" x 11".

Ferrari Serial Numbers Part II

Ferrari Serial Numbers Part II is the only publicly available Ferrari Serial Number database. The title covers the even numbered chassis (racing cars) through serial number 1050. Compiled in 1989 by preeminent Ferrari Historians Hilary Raab and Dyke Ridgley, the title is the definitive serial number database. The edition presented here is unchanged from the original 1989 version and has not been updated. While some of the information regarding the cars has subsequently changed, the title is still a unique and invaluable reference work for the serious Ferrari Historian. The companion title, "Ferrari Serial Numbers Part I", covers the odd numbered chassis (road cars) to serial number 21399.

Author: Hilary A. Raab. **Pages:** 128. **Dimensions:** 8.1/4" x 11".

Ferrari Owner's Handbook

This edition is presented unchanged from the original 1961 edition, and as before: Is a compilation of specifications and statistical data as well as factory drawings. Though it is in no manner an attempt to encompass every model of Ferrari built, it is, however, an attempt to present a cross-section of the best, and most famous Ferraris built since 1948. The reader will find specifications - presented in chronological order, action photos, sales promotion photos, candid pit-side photos, driving experiences, maintenance data, repair data, timing charts, lubrication charts, wiring diagrams, and cut-away drawings which will aid the Ferrari owner and enthusiast alike.

Author: Veloce Press – Clymer. **Pages:** 174. **Dimensions:** 7" x 10".

Ferrari: Operating, Maintenance and Services Handbooks 1948-1963

A compilation of technical data specific to the 166 Inter & Mille Miglia, 195 Inter, 212 Export & Inter, 340 America, 250 Mille Miglia, 340 Mille Miglia, 342 America, 500 Mondial, 750 Monza, 4 & 412 (6-Cylinder), 250 Granturismo & 250GT/E coupe 2+2 and other similar models. Includes Weber carburetor data sheets and Magneti Marelli electrical component drawings.

Author: Richard F. Merritt. **Pages:** 320. **Dimensions:** 10 3/4" x 8 1/4".

Ferrari Brochures and Sales Literature 1946-1967

The ultimate reference for early Ferrari brochures and sales literature, this edition is presented unchanged from the original 1976 edition. This should be considered a companion volume to Randall Baselt's book, which continues on covering the later brochures and sales literature from 1968 through 1989.

Author: Richard F. Merritt. **Pages:** 286. **Dimensions:** 10 3/4" x 8 1/4".

Ferrari Brochures and Sales Literature 1968-1989

Although this is not a Veloce Press publication, we are the distributor for this book. 1200 black & white illustrations. This book is a continuation of Dick Merritt's similar work, and should be considered to be a companion volume

Author: Randall Baselt. **Pages:** 354. **Dimensions:** 10 3/4" x 8 1/4".

Ferrari 250/GT Service and Maintenance

A compilation of technical information and data to aid in the service, maintenance, care and repair of the Ferrari 250GT, 250GTE, 250GTL, 250SWB and other similar models.

Author: Jim Riff. **Pages:** 116. **Dimensions:** 8 1/4" x 11".

Ferrari Guide to Performance

Allen S. Bishop's book covers tuning and maintenance hints on virtually all V-12 and early V-8 Ferraris. A wealth of information by one of California's top restorers, the Ferrari Guide to Performance also includes a step by step illustrated feature on how to rebuild the famous Weber carburetors used on most V-12 Ferraris. Originally published in 1987, VelocePress is pleased to bring this invaluable resource back into print.

Author: Allen S. Bishop. **Pages** 141. **Dimensions:** 7.5" x 9.25".

Ferrari Spyder California

Subtitled: A Ferrari Of Particular Distinction. Originally published in 1976, the VelocePress edition presented here is unchanged from the original version and has not been updated. This landscape format book provides the reader with an in-depth analysis of the Ferrari Spyder racing and road cars (1958-1962).

Author: George M. Carrick. **Pages:** 76. **Dimensions:** 10 3/4" x 8 1/4".

Ferrari Berlinetta Lusso

Subtitled: A Ferrari Of Unusual Elegance. Originally published in 1978, this book provides the reader with an in-depth analysis of the Ferrari Lusso (1962-1964). The VelocePress edition presented here is unchanged from the original and has not been updated. However, it has been re-formatted from the original "landscape" orientation into a more conventional "portrait" format.

Author: Kurt H. Miska. **Pages:** 118. **Dimensions:** 7" x 10".

Many more titles of interest to the classic automobile and motorcycle enthusiast available at ~ www.VelocePress.com
Please check our website or contact your dealer for more information

Printed in the United States
142434LV00003B/3/A